AF271511

Munchies for Salespeople II

Munchies for Salespeople II

More Sales Tips You Can Sink Your Teeth Into

From IAS Training's Weekly Letter
"Sales Insight"

Developed and Written by
Brad Huisken

Copyright © 2012 by Brad Huisken
All rights reserved.

No part of this work may be reproduced or transmitted in
any form by any means, electronic or mechanical,
including photocopying and recording, or by any
information storage or retrieval system, except as may be
expressly permitted by the 1976 Copyright Act or in
writing by the publisher. Requests for such permission
should be addressed to:

IAS Training
6655 West Jewell Ave
Suite 210
Lakewood, CO 80232
303-936-9353
800-248-7703
www.iastraining.com
info@iastraining.com

Huisken, Brad
    Munchies for Salespeople II:
    More Sales Tips You Can Sink Your Teeth Into
    ISBN   978-0-9651069-7-9

Cover Design by – Mark Mulvaney
Interior Design by – Joe Morrone

Printed in the United States of America
10 9 8 7 6 5 4 3 2 1

Forward

Brad Huisken has written a great book that explains management's role in building a significant culture among work groups at any level, particularly at the store level. The book, however, is much more than an easily understood tactical book for store management; it is also a book about leadership and the impact of positive leadership on store teams.

Over the years, I have read many quotes about leadership and the role of leadership in successful business entities. My favorite is: *The most powerful force on earth is a human engaged in meaningful work.* And there is another equally impactful quote that reads: *Select (team members)with science and hold (work teams) together with leadership and culture.*

Huisken's book explains how great managers can engage the thoughts and actions of their team members to create a meaningful culture that will enhance the success of a company for a very long time. Great cultures have constant, positive and actionable communication that must be delivered by management. This book provides great material and inspiration about how to communicate and coach subordinates at all levels. It is all about positive leadership and the impact of that leadership on the culture of a successful business.

I have learned through observations and study that the deliberate creation of a
unique company culture is a strategic advantage for any business. The short chapters in Brad's book provide material about how to go to create a positive culture that can be shared in a timely and effective manner with everyone in a company, *thereby raising the significance level of the company.*

Leading gives one the chance to be successful as well as significant. The difference between the two is that when you die, your success comes to an end. When you are significant you continue to help others be successful long after you are gone. Significance can last many life times. Brads book will enhance the success of your business model and help you be significant to your team for a very long time.

Brad, Great Job!

John Thedford
Author
Smart Moves Management – Cultivating World Class People and Profits

Introduction

Occasionally, we all need a shot in the arm so to speak, a bit of motivation or inspirational lift to get us going on the right track. While you may not want to or have the time to read an entire book to get it, a short burst of energy, would be sufficient. This book was compiled with that very thought in mind. The ideas, concepts, strategies, and techniques are written in short, easy to read and easy to find messages. To support this goal, the book has been designed so that all of the ideas are condensed into one page.

Munchies for Salespeople II: More Sales Tips You Can Sink Your Teeth Into, is composed of 140 thoughts and ideas. You can focus on one idea per day, week, or month. You can read the book from cover to cover pointing out certain ideas or areas of importance that you want to refer back to in the future. This book is for you, use it however you wish, write in it, highlight parts of it, re-read it, but whatever you do, use it. I hope you find the tips and strategies helpful in your pursuit to reach success in your chosen career of sales.

Dedication

This book is dedicated to my grandchildren Lindsay Huisken, Kody Huisken, Leyton Kyelberg, Avery Huisken, Emma Kyelberg & Bennett Huisken. You will see some photos of "the grandkids" throughout this book. Words cannot express the joy and the love that you have given me in your short lives. Everyday you put a smile on my face, and love in my heart, no matter whether I am with you or not. I am so proud of each and every one of you. Remember life is simply a matter of choices and decisions. Always make choices and decisions that would make your Grandpa, (Poppi, Bampu) and Grandma proud. I know you will be successful in your lives no matter what you pursue. It won't be easy! It will take a lot of hard work, dedication, perseverance, commitment, drive, and self determinism. All attributes that I can already see in each and every one of you. I love you!

Acknowledgments

Whenever taking on a monumental task like writing a book, there are always numerous people that need to be recognized for their contribution, and this book is no different. There have been dozens of people involved in the completion, publishing, and distribution of this book. While I cannot name them all, I do want to acknowledge the major contributors.

First, I would like to thank my wife, Rainie, who has stood by me for the past 40 years while I traveled around the world realizing my dreams and achieving my goals. In addition she not only helped insert the pictures and formatted the book, she has also contributed a number of the writings published in this book, not to mention her ability to take my thoughts and words and put them into a language most can understand. Additionally, I want to thank my sons David and Brice and my daughter Dina, for their ideas and input to this book. I want them to know how very much I appreciate their support, love, and understanding they have shown over the years as I have missed many important days in their lives to pursue my dreams. I want them to know I was there in spirit and they were always number one in my heart as I have done this for all of us in order to help realize our dreams and provide for a comfortable life for all of us.

I would also like to acknowledge and thank my parents, Carol Campbell and George Huisken and stepparents, Patricia Huisken and Foster Campbell. The principles, values, work ethic, and disciplines that they taught me through my life have been monumental. Words cannot express my sincere appreciation and gratitude for the impact they have had on all aspects of my life.

I also want to acknowledge and thank my nephew, Joe Morrone, for the hours he spent on the computer choosing the articles and researching the quotes and his major contribution to this book. To my daughter in-law, Kate Huisken, there are no words to express my gratitude for all her help in the creation of this work.

The graphic art design for the cover of this book is the fine work of Mark Mulvaney. I sincerely appreciate his creative contributions for this book as well as our other training materials. I further want to thank John Thedford, Author of the book Smart Moves Management, Cultivating World-Class People and Profits, for his advice and contribution in writing the forward to this book for me. I would also like to recognize the friends, business professionals, and acquaintances that took the time to read an advance copy of Munchies for Salespeople and contributed quotes.

Last, but not least, I would like to thank the many salespeople who have given me the opportunity to learn from them. Regardless of whether they are the bad examples that I refer to throughout these articles, or the good examples, I want them to know I definitely empathize with the time and effort they put into their job. I also recognize they are working in one of the greatest professions on earth, *SALES*.

FINAO – Brad Huisken

Table of Contents

We never lead with product; we lead with need.

Zig Ziglar

A Message To Sales People!

As a salesperson you are on the front line. You are the one that can make or break a business. The reason is that you are the first, and in many cases, the only person that the customer has any contact with from your company. You are the first and last impression that the customer has. I have talked many times about the real goal of a sales presentation; that is to: develop personal trade, repeat business and referral business. The goal of a salesperson isn't simply to make a sale; it goes deeper than that. Therefore the following is a definition of the job of a salesperson:

> One that <u>causes</u> the exchange of ownership of a product or service based upon the customer's <u>wants</u> and <u>needs</u> with <u>integrity</u>!

Let's look at each of the underlined words: Causes – I believe that single handedly a salesperson can cause the success or failure of a company and an individual sales presentation. Every day you make decisions that will cause a customer to buy or not buy. Every day you make the decision to walk a customer or give it a 100% effort to attempt to sell them. You will cause a customer to buy add-on items or to not buy any additional goods. You will cause a customer to come back and buy from you again and you will cause a customer to actually recommend you and your company to others. You can and will make or break a sales organization.

Sell based on the customer's wants and needs: The most successful salespeople are capable of asking questions to determine specifically each customer's wants and needs. Each and every customer is different and in order to maximize the selling opportunity you must sell based on the reason that the customer wants and needs to buy.

A leader is a dealer in hope.

Napoleon Bonaparte

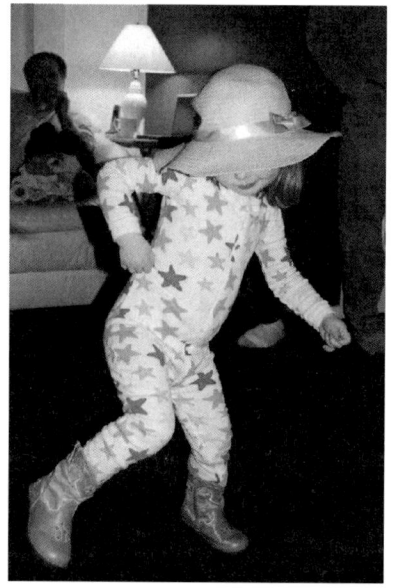

A Message To Sales Managers!

The majority of sales managers that I meet have many more responsibilities other than the sales management of the sales people. Many times, it seems as though those tasks or responsibilities tend to get in the way of the primary function of a sales manager. It takes discipline, delegation and a concentrated effort to get the whole job done. In too many situations, the salespeople are the ones who suffer or get put on the back burner until all the other tasks are done. In some cases the other tasks will never be complete. To that end I thought I would detail the primary job responsibility of a sales manager. That is to:

> Provide the leadership, knowledge, training, incentives and consequences to recruit, hire, train, develop and maintain a successful sales staff.

The preceding definition certainly isn't an easy job to accomplish. As a matter of fact, the job will never be done. You will be in the business of recruiting, hiring and training for as long as you have the position. However, the goal has to be to have a completely trained staff that is capable of maximizing each and every selling opportunity that they have available. Further a completely trained sales staff will be capable of creating sales opportunities through various other means as well.

My suggestion is to break down each and every word of the definition of a sales manager and do a little bit of a self-evaluation. Ask yourself; are you providing leadership and exactly what is leadership? Are you providing the knowledge and training that your salespeople need in order to be successful? Are you providing incentives and both positive and negative consequences through running a disciplined sales organization? Are you managing based on objective information rather than opinion or subjective information? In other words, are you giving your people all of the tools that they need to be successful, thus creating your own success?

There is only one rule to being a good talker -
learn to listen.

Christopher Morley

You Can't Fake It!

We are all guilty, we have all committed the act and if you are an honest person you can't really deny it. I am not proud of it and I certainly wouldn't encourage others to participate. I know that I have been caught on numerous occasions, just today as a matter of fact. I do it to my wife, my children, my co-workers, my friends and even my parents. But hey, it happens. What is it? At one time or another I would guess that you have been caught faking it. What do I mean by faking it? I mean not giving your complete and total attention to someone who is speaking with you. Sometimes a person can have a fifteen-minute conversation with me and after it is over, I wonder what we were just talking about. My wife can tell me something about our children and want my opinion, and I have no idea what she just said. A co-worker can ask me a question expecting some profound answer and I can't give one because I don't know what they said to me. Something even worse is at, or near the end of a conversation, you are asked a question and you have no idea what the question is or how it should be answered, so you *fake it*.

If I have learned anything over time it is that when you fake it you will lose 95% of the time. You'll answer the wrong question, give an opinion regarding the wrong subject, or worst of all you will have to admit that you weren't listening. A fate worse than many others I can think of because you may be perceived as uncaring, selfish, or just plain rude.

We are all human beings and we are all guilty of communication blunders from time to time. I hope that your friends, family and co-workers are forgiving. However, your customers may not be. Your customers may simply leave, **empty handed**, when you are not giving them your complete and undivided attention. The price for not paying attention is a heavy one to bear. Work on giving everyone, including your customers, the attention they deserve. If you practice listening to your family, friends, and co-workers, it will become a habit that carries over to your customers. Result – better personal relationships and MORE SALES!

It takes a great deal of living to get a little deal of learning.

John Ruskin

Where's The Money?

Recently I had the opportunity to meet a young part-time salesperson. This person is working in a retail store through high school to make some extra money and to help her decide what career path she should take. Through our conversation this person asked me an interesting question. The question was:

"Where do you think the opportunity is to make money or what occupation do you think is going to offer the best opportunity for me to live a fruitful life?

When you really think about it, there is not a single answer. I know many people who don't, or haven't, fulfilled the opportunity that they have been given. I know others who seem to have been born with a silver spoon, the type of people that no matter what they do, they are successful. There are others that have to work very hard at success and are never satisfied with the level of success that they have achieved. Then there are other people who just coast along and live their life hand to mouth. Every one of us is different with varying goals, expectations and dreams.

The only common denominator that I can think of for anyone looking for where the money is comes in three words. The words being:

Knowledge, Self-determination & Passion.

No matter what profession a person chooses to pursue, if they possess a passion for the business, have the self-determination to not settle for average results, and constantly seek knowledge, and then apply that knowledge, any profession can reap the rewards of a fruitful, successful professional life.
The sales profession is no different. Salespeople can be the lowest paid people or the highest paid people. The choice is yours to make!

We miss 100% of the sales we don't ask for.

Zig Ziglar

Don't Be Afraid To Ask For It

We have spent the past ten to twenty years trying to distance ourselves from the stereotype that salespeople are pushy and only interested in making a sale to increase their commissions. While I agree with the intent and firmly believe that the basis for any professional salesperson is customer service, I do find it necessary to make the point that there is a difference between being pushy and giving the customer what they want or need.

The point is that at some stage in the selling process, you need to ask for the sale, and not expect the customer to do it for you. I have some friends who were recently in the market for a mini-van and proceeded to a local dealership. It was a Saturday and they were anxious to buy. They found a van that they wanted and were ready to start talking about specifics such as, financing, trade-in value, and so on. The dealership told them that because it was Saturday they would not be able to get an answer on financing until Tuesday, maybe Wednesday. They were ready to buy that day and the salesperson missed the signs. My friends were so disenchanted with the experience that they took their business elsewhere.

Within four hours after finding a van they liked at another dealership, they drove home in their new mode of transportation. The dealership they finally bought from showed those four different vans, went over all financing options, and had the deal done that night. The dealership had three different people working on all aspects of the sale and did everything they could to satisfy the requirements of the customer.

There is a distinct difference between a pushy salesperson and one that gives the customer what they want. In the first scenario, my friends were ready to buy, but the salesman was apparently not ready to sell, as he asked them to come back in a few days when they could go over financing possibilities. That approach certainly is not pushy but it is also completely ineffective. In the second scenario, the salespeople found out what my friends wanted, and then worked with them to find a deal that would work for them. Finding out what your customers need and working with them to fulfill those needs is not pushy; on the contrary, it is great customer service. Providing great customer service is not pushy, it is professional.

Education comes from within; you get by effort and struggle and thought.

Napoleon Hill

You Get Out What You Put In!

A touch of fall is in the air, can you feel it? I did not realize it, considering it has been summer like temperatures everyday for who knows how long, no matter where I am. However, as I was driving to the office the other morning, I noticed kids walking to school. That, along with my grandkids starting school recently, got me thinking about education and the benefits that it can provide. For a lot of us, we think of education as something that we take part in while we are young and then apply to our chosen profession when we are older.

I believe that real education and learning is a lifelong process that should never end. Naturally, I turn my thinking to the field of sales, education, and the effects of ongoing education in our field. The answers are too numerous to cover in one article, but I think I can give you an idea of what I am talking about.

As we discussed in the last article, technology is always changing and it takes constant attention to stay up on those advances. Well, that is a part of the educational process for salespeople. If you are familiar with the technology that assists you, then the better your presentations will be and you will hear "I'll take it" more frequently.

Sales, as with any other field, are always changing. There are always new techniques, a new closing strategy, or new customer service ideas. The professional salesperson is constantly reading or attending seminars to learn about those things that will make them sell just one more product or close just one more deal. Yet, unlike school, no one is going to force you to take the class on the new product line. No one is going to demand that you read the hot article about how to close a deal when no one else can.

This time, it is completely up to you. You will get out of it what you put into it, if you put forth the effort and constantly keep up on the ever-changing field of sales. The educational process is a never-ending one and I hope you are taking full advantage of the training and other educational opportunities available to you. As for all of the students returning to school, have a great year!

"A good coach will hold the team accountable for both their actions and their results."
Catherine Pulsifer,

Accountability

We've spent some time now talking about goals, setting goals for both your individual salespeople and for your team as a whole. We've also talked about how to track progress toward the goals and coaching when the goals are not being met. Today I want to move on to a subject that goes hand in hand with goals, and that is **accountability.**

Simply put, accountability is ensuring that the people on your sales team are working toward, and ultimately meeting, the goals that you have set for them. It is a way of keeping score in order to track the progress in reaching the goals, both by company and individual. If people are not aware of how they are doing in relationship to goals and standards that you have set, then how can you expect them to succeed?

Every company has numbers that they set based on many factors, but there are some questions you can ask yourself to assist you in holding your staff accountable.

Why should salespeople be held accountable to numbers? As we've all ready touched on, having set goals and numbers is the only real way to track progress. Imagine if a college student just went to class but never had to be graded. There is no way of knowing if they've learned and retained the information. A salesperson can be perfect in presentation and closing techniques, but if they are not actually selling, then what are they offering the company?

What numbers should you track? This is really a question that needs to be answered by each individual sales manager. However, tracking your sales, sales to goal, add-ons, average sale, transactions per hour and Closing Ratio are the primary numbers that I suggest.

Total sales are a result of other actions. As we've discussed before, you cannot coach total sales but you can coach the actions the lead to the sales result. If a salesperson is not reaching their goals because they cannot close, then you provide additional training on closing techniques.

Setting goals is the first part of accountability, but that must be followed by holding people accountable to reaching the goals. By doing so, you will increase the total sales of each salesperson and sales as a whole.

"It is not only what we do, but also what we do not do, for which we are accountable. "

- Moliere

Accountability-Part 2

We talked a lot about accountability the last time we were together and the numbers you should use in order to hold people accountable. There is one number; however, that is more important than any other number, the number being the **closing ratio average or CRA.** The CRA will give you a true measure of where you are and help you to reach higher levels of success. In other words, the CRA is as important in the field of sales as the win/loss record is in sports.

A football team does not know truly how it has done until the final score, team A can have more yards and dominate field position, but if team B scores more points, then it is team B that is viewed as successful. In selling terms, if a salesperson's CRA is 20% then imagine the increase in revenue if that same salesperson increases their CRA to 30%. Can you think of any salesperson who would not want 50% more in sales and/or commissions?

Calculating CRA is fairly simple-write a chicken scratch on a piece of paper for every opportunity that you have. At the end of the day you will know how many opportunities you had, then you divide the numbers of sales you had by the number of opportunities. For example, if you had 23 opportunities in a given day and made 9 sales then your CRA would be 39.13%.

Accountability numbers like CRA must be tracked daily and totaled on a weekly and monthly basis: It is vital that you track numbers as you go, waiting to do everything at the end of the day, week or at the end of the month with produce inaccuracies that will in turn produce false information. It will take you no more than five or ten minutes to tally and examine your numbers daily; take the time. It will be worth it.

Individual salespeople must calculate their individual numbers: While the sales manager is capable of tracking everyone's numbers, the salesperson themselves should be tracking their own numbers. The sales manager has enough to do without having to track everyone's numbers. Plus, it gives the salesperson an idea of how they are doing, where they need to improve and what is working. In short, it gives the individual salespeople a tool to hold themselves accountable.

Create an atmosphere for the spirit. The spirit must be present.

Richard G. Scott

ATMOSPHERE

I was recently walking through a mall doing some early Christmas shopping and as usual, I noticed a few things in relation to the field of sales. What can I say, it's an occupational hazard. The one thing that really stuck in my mind over the rest this time was the word *atmosphere*. Obviously at this time of year, the atmosphere of all the stores is one of excitement and activity. Why do you think that is? Why do you think stores decorate the way they do and try to capture the holiday season? I am sure part of it is just the idea that it is the holidays but I believe there is more to it.

The term "buying environment" comes to mind. Now granted people are more apt to shop and buy at this time of year, but stores do an excellent job of creating an atmosphere that is conducive to buying. They know that this is the busiest time of year for most retailers, so they are going to do their best to take advantage of it. My question is: why don't salespeople take advantage of what a buying environment can provide more often?

If you walk into an electronics store in December, it is pretty apparent what time of year it is and that they want you to buy. However, if you walk into the same store in May, is the atmosphere the same? Now not everything can match the energy of the holidays, but by taking the time to create a buying environment more often can lead to increased sales.

For example, spring is a season that many people look forward to after the long winter. They want to get outside, plant, or go camping. If people are looking to be outside, then why not take advantage of that with a sidewalk sale. Maybe combine that with a BBQ for anyone who comes between a set time and perhaps a class on setting up a tent.

You get the idea! I just see so much excitement and environments that are set up for the customer to say, "I'll take it" at this time of year and I wonder why salespeople would not take more advantage of that? Take the time to create a buying atmosphere and I think your customers will reward your efforts.

Destiny is no matter of chance. It's a matter of choice: it is not a thing to be waited for; it is a thing to be achieved.

William Jennings Bryan

YOUR DESTINY IS YOUR DECISION

One of the things that I appreciate the most about our profession as salespeople is that we control our own destiny. As a salesperson, you alone wake up every morning and choose what the outcome of the day will be. You alone can decide if you are going to repeat the actions of the past or look for new and better ways to do your job. You alone control your attitude, enthusiasm, and commitment.

Just as a company has to reinvent itself on a regular basis, so must you, the sales professional. Look at yourself and your profession as a one-person organization. You are a one-person sales organization that has the capability to make as much or as little money as you decide you want to make. You can decide for yourself if you are going to be an entrepreneur or an employee. You can be a success or a failure. You can excel or remain average. You can lead a great life or you can lead a bad life. All these decisions are yours and yours alone. You can lead, follow, or get out of the way; it's your choice. Whatever the choice, they all take the exact same time commitment.

As a one-man sales operation, you need to be proactive rather than reactive. As an entrepreneur you need to continually ask yourself several questions, get the answers, and then make the changes necessary. Those questions are:

- Where are my skills lacking?
- What further knowledge do I need?
- What trends do I need to watch in my industry?
- What is my competition doing (internally and externally)?
- What information do I lack?
- What training do I need?
- What can I do to improve?
- Why do people buy, or not buy, from me?

You alone control your destiny. What other profession allows for that much control involving your destiny?

You cannot truly listen to anyone and do anything
else at the same time.

M. Scott Peck

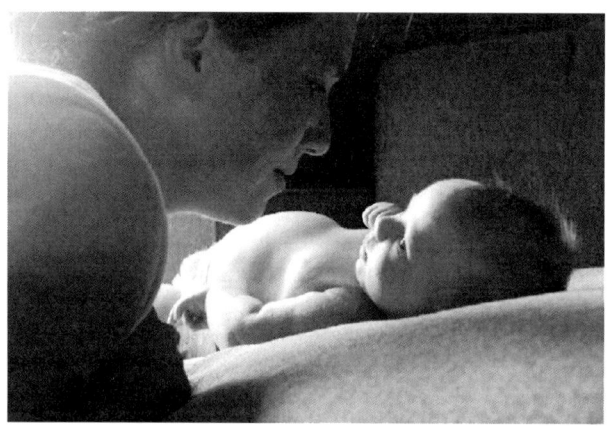

BUYING SIGNS

I would like to take this opportunity to re-visit the art of recognizing and acting on buying signs. We all have a good idea of what a buying sign entails but for our purposes, we will define it as when a customer gives you a sign that they are ready to buy. It could be something like the customer saying, "When can you deliver?" or something a little more subtle like, "I really like it but..." Both of these statements should be immediate cues to the professional salesperson that the customer is ready to buy.

Today, though, I want to talk less about how to recognize a buying sign and more about the consequences of failing to. I would like to share a story with you that a friend of mine experienced and later shared with me. He was in the market for a new set of golf clubs, had been shopping around for two or three weeks, and had a good idea of what he wanted. He finally found himself at a local sporting goods store and found a set that he really liked and began talking with the salesperson.

As the conversation progressed, my friend became increasingly convinced this was the set of clubs he had been looking for. He tried them out by hitting balls into a net and confirmed what he thought, that he really liked the feel of the clubs. He told the salesperson that he liked the set and asked about the price. (Buying sign!) The salesperson proceeded to tell my friend about the new shafts on the clubs. My friend then asked if he could purchase a putter as a part of the set. (Buying sign!) Once again, the salesperson went back into the presentation. This went on for a couple more minutes and finally my friend told the salesperson the he would look around and get back to him.

This salesperson missed a sale because he just did not recognize the buying signs. The salesperson did their job, they made the sale, but they failed to complete the sale. He already had sold the golf clubs, and then bought them back because of his inability to see my friend was ready to buy. Do not give up a sale because you are trying to sell something to a customer that has all ready said, "I'll take it!"

If you don't take care of your customers someone else will.

Unknown

What is Customer Service?

What does customer service mean to you? What is customer service? My guess is you are all giving some answer and that they are all similar, yet different. My guess is also that you are all right in one form or another. There is no simple explanation of what customer service is or even less of an explanation of what quality customer service entails. I know what customer service is and is not, which leads me to the meat of this article.

We all know about the price of gas, and how it has affected each of us one way or another. I understand that gas stations have little control over the price per gallon and have to find other ways to compete for their share of the marketplace. I shared with you the story of a local station that gave away a small cup of coffee to every customer who filled their tanks as a way to lure customers to buy their gas. That is customer service! They are providing a benefit to me because I chose their product over the station across the street. They understood that offering free coffee would not change the price of gas, but the added benefit might make it less painful.

What is not customer service is when the customer has to pay to receive the service. The other day I was out driving and noticed that I needed gas. As I approached an intersection, I saw two stations caddy corner from one another. To my surprise, one was 10 cents higher than its competitor was. I found that to be curious. How could there be such a big difference? Who in their right mind would pick the one that was 10 cents higher? The curiosity got the better of me so I stopped and asked why they charged 10 cents more than the station across the street. I was told they do that in order to offer "full service" and call it "customer service." I said to the attendant, "That is not customer service; you are providing an additional service that you are charging for. It would only be a customer service if you were using it as a way to attract customers to your store in order to offset the high price of gas."

In short, customer service is a tool to get customers to choose your products over your competitors, not as another way to make a profit.

Don't look back: Something may be gaining on you.

Satchel Paige

BAD DAYS-WE ALL HAVE THEM

Do you ever have a bad day? Of course you do; we all do. Maybe you had an argument with your spouse, the kids are in trouble at school, you just found out about an unexpected expense, or you just woke up in a lousy mood. Whatever the reason, it is naïve to believe that anyone can be in a great mood and on top of his or her game every single day. However, that is what I am going to ask of you.

As we all know, the sales business is less about sales and more about the relationships that you develop and maintain throughout the years. In order to develop those relationships, customers, particularly new customers, must begin to develop a level of trust with you as the salesperson. If you are in a grumpy mood and short with a potential repeat customer, then you are not only doing them a disservice, but you are also doing a disservice to yourself. Even if that customer does end up buying from you and is completely satisfied with what they bought, do you think they are coming back? My guess is probably not, and they are probably telling all of their friends about the great product they bought, but what a lousy experience it was with a grouchy salesperson.

A few days ago, I took my car for some repairs and received great customer service from beginning to end. I received updates on the progress and they even came in under the price they quoted. I was pleased right up until the point that I went to get in my car. An attendant was assigned to retrieve my car and bring it to me. As I am getting into my car I say thank you and the attendant under his breath says, "How hard is it for customers to go get their own cars?" I've worked with this person long enough to know he was probably just having a rough day but that does not change the fact that I drove away with an unsatisfied feeling, even though everything else was great.

It is not always easy to leave our personal problems in our personal lives, but your potential customers do not care if you spilled coffee all over your new suit today. They deserve your best efforts because even though you will be in a better mood tomorrow, they are here today.

*Culture is like wealth; it makes us more ourselves,
it enables us to express ourselves.*

Phillip Gilbert Hamerton

What Is The Culture!

What culture does your company have? Is it a Sales Culture, Merchandise Culture, Operations Culture, Repair/Service Culture, etc? In other words when someone mentions the name of your company, what is the first thing they think of? Is it that you have a great selection of merchandise? Is it that you do great repair work? I hope they are thinking what great **people** you have that will do anything to help service the customer's needs, because that is a sales driven organization.

A sales driven organization is a company that from top to bottom, realizes that they are in the sales business. Whether the customer was to speak to the accounting person, janitor, receptionist, repairperson, salesperson or the owner, everyone would have the customer's best interest in mind. Too often I see organizations where the repair department looks at customers as a pain. I see accounting people that answer phones and treat the person on the other end as a burden, rather than an asset.

The minute that everyone in the organization realizes that the only reason any position exists in any company is because of the customer, is the minute you become a sales driven organization. If you didn't have sales would you need anyone to account for inventory and money? If you didn't have any customers, would you really need a buying department? Without customers to buy products, would you really need a repair department?

Now go a step further. Has everyone in the organization been trained to provide exceptional customer service? Trained to communicate (how to speak with a customer), how to go the extra mile, to provide exchange in abundance, that the customer is always right. Have they been taught how to handle delicate situations, how to handle returns, exchanges, defective merchandise, etc. I would hope the answer is "Yes" because you never know to whom or when a customer may talk to a given employee. No matter what position they hold, they are all in sales and represent you and your company.

The most basic of all human needs is the need to understand and be understood. The best way to understand people is to listen to them.

Ralph Nichols

ARE YOU LISTENING?

I can't say it enough; you need to listen to your customers. They will give you all the information you need to begin a relationship with them. Find out exactly what they want, why they want it, any potential add-on items and to complete the sale when you really hear what a customer is saying. Even if the sale doesn't happen today, at the very least you establish the relationship, which will increase your chances of making a sale in the foreseeable future. Establishing a relationship requires LISTENING, HEARING and ACTING based on what your customer tells you, not what you want to hear.

Listening is an art, and requires practice. You can listen to someone and hear every word they say and still not acquire the information you need. This is a common problem in listening and is similar to not seeing the big picture when looking at someone. We can look at someone and make a decision about them, like what we think of them, where we would assume they live, and various other stereotypes. We can do the same thing when we listen, assume we know what they want by *listening* to only portions of what they are saying even though we *heard* every word. This is, in a sense, stereotyping what we hear and defeating our purpose of listening in the first place. The *art* comes in when we pay attention to every word we heard and read between the lines. This aids in leading us to ask the right questions and obtain critical information in order to establish a relationship with our customer and set the groundwork for making a sale.

I think we could honestly admit we are all guilty of not listening at times. Have you ever thought you were listening to someone so intently that you knew exactly what they wanted only to find out it was totally opposite of what you thought? My wife could tell you this has happened between us. Like the time my wife said, "I would like to have one carat diamond earrings that sparkle as much as my diamond necklace." I heard "I would like to have one carat diamond earrings to go with my diamond necklace." No doubt a completely different message was received as that which was delivered. The minute I heard 1 carat my attention was on the 1 carat, not the sparkle. Great listening requires unbiased hearing and the ability to pick up what the customer is telling you by listening to and hearing every word. Are you listening?

Without goals, and plans to reach them, you are like a ship that set sail with no destination.

Fitzhugh Dodson

Up The Down Escalator!

Do you ever feel like you are spending your life, including your career, trying to go up the down escalator? Does it seem as though all the forces are driving against you? Do you feel as though the rest of the world is easily going up while you are struggling just to maintain your position, much less get ahead? Life and career, including the profession of sales, have a unique comparison with the struggle of fighting opposing forces in order to get ahead.

If you are stuck on the down escalator trying to go up, you have several choices. You can give into the opposing forces and simply give up. You can keep exerting the same energy as the escalator and simply maintain your position. You can wait for the escalator to stop, seeing who will be first to give into defeat. You can exert more energy and move faster than the escalator itself, or you can get off the escalator and look for another one that is heading in the right direction.

Realistically, if you want to accomplish your goals, there are only two approaches. Get off the escalator and find one that is heading the same direction as you want to go, or exert more energy and achieve the ultimate goal of reaching the top no matter what the opposing forces may be. Finding another escalator may be a difficult chore as you never know where and when you might find it. To save time and to reach the top in the shortest amount of time I suggest, "dam the torpedoes full speed ahead."

In our personal life and our business life, we have choices that we need to make every day. We can stop, stay the same, wait, or give it all we have got. No matter what opposing forces we might face, ultimately we are in complete control of our own destiny. Through extra effort and perseverance we can achieve anything we want to achieve if we want it bad enough. Your destiny is in your own hands. What you do with it is up to you.

A mind is like a parachute. It doesn't work if it's not open.

Frank Zappa

A Parachute Is Like A Brain!

A parachute is like a brain in that it only works when it is completely open. A closed parachute does you absolutely no good when you are free falling through the sky. It is an open parachute that will mean the difference between a successful jump and ___, well you get the picture. Can't the same thing be said about the brain? An open mind will be the difference between a successful endeavor and a failed attempt.

When your mind is open, you are able to learn new things, to experiment with new ideas or techniques and to learn and grow. It is the narrow or closed-minded individual that becomes complacent. When complacency sets in, it is very difficult, if not impossible, to turn things around. This is what could be called "burn-out". There is no greater enemy to a salesperson, or anybody for that matter, than complacency or closed mindedness.

With all the changes, technological advances, new information, and access to these tools that is becoming available a person that doesn't, or will not, take advantage of these valuable tools is foolish. Look around at other companies. Look at, read, and study the trade journals. Shop other companies or stores that aren't necessarily in your industry to see what other segments of your field are doing. Get up to speed on the internet and the wealth of information available to you in your industry. No one can afford to sit back and wait for ideas and knowledge to come to them. You have to go out and aggressively pursue the knowledge that is at your fingertips.

An open mind will grow and flourish. A closed mind, like a closed parachute, is heading for disaster. I encourage you to pull the ripcord on your brain and avoid a freefall into the future. From up here the opportunities are endless, it all depends on your willingness to learn and grow.

The customer is why you go to work, if they go away you do too.

David Haverford

UPSET CUSTOMER – BAD EXAMPLE

If you are in this field longer than five minutes, then chances are good that you are going to encounter your share of upset or unhappy customers. We have talked in the past about how to deal with upset customers and have given you the techniques needed. So I do not want to rehash that, but I do want to share with you two different experiences that will illustrate what not to do and what to do.

The first of these I witnessed while I was shopping at an electronics store with a friend of mine, who was there to have a system installed. As we were walking around the store, a salesperson came out and told my friend that they would be unable to install the system he bought and if he really wanted it, he would have to spend a great deal more money for what he wanted. If you knew my friend, you would know that he does his homework when it comes to major purchases and he knew that the salesperson was not telling him the whole truth. Therefore, he called him on it and said that he believed it could be done exactly the way they had talked about, and asked the salesperson to either complete the work or he would take his business elsewhere. To my friend's dismay, the salesperson said that they would only do it the way he had described and said that any company that would do it any other way is crazy. We got into my friend's car and headed for a different store and they performed the installation exactly the way my friend wanted, and he has had zero problems since.

Now my friend was not particularly upset in the true sense that we all think about when we hear the term upset customer. However, it still provides an excellent example of a customer interaction that leaves a great deal to be desired. The salesperson showed a complete lack of respect for my friend and his knowledge of exactly what he wanted. Certainly, in many cases, the salesperson is the expert in the field but that does not mean you do not listen and work with your customers. The best salesperson-customer relationships are the ones when they work together to meet the needs and desires of said customer. Do not be afraid to listen. Next time, I will share a more positive experience in dealing with an upset customer.

One customer well taken care of could be more valuable than $10,000.00 worth of advertising.

Jim Robin

UPSET CUSTOMER – GOOD EXAMPLE

Last time we discussed an example of how not to deal with an upset customer and gave you an idea of a poor interaction between a customer and a salesperson. This time, happily, will have a much more positive spin or at least the outcome is more positive.

A nephew of mine, who has Cerebral Palsy, told this particular example to me. He talks a little different, but is smart as a whip and has a job and a family just like the rest of us. I only mention this to you to better set up the story I am going to share with you.

A few years ago, my nephew decided to order a pizza for dinner. When the person at the pizza place answered the phone and said, "May I help you," that is when it all began. My nephew started to order, only to hear the person on the other end of the line start to mock the way he was talking. Generally, my nephew lets stuff like that go but he was not having the greatest of weeks and he decided enough is enough. He jumped in his car and drove to the pizza place where he asked to speak to a manager. He shared the above story with the manager and the following is an excellent example in dealing with an upset customer.

The first thing that the manager did was talk to the employee in private and five minutes later the manager came out and asked my nephew to wait a couple more minutes. After those two minutes, the manager emerged with two large pizzas and an order of bread. The manager handed all of it to my nephew and said please accept my apology and these pizzas on the house. My nephew felt as though his concerns were addressed and the manager made it right. Had nothing else happened, my nephew would have been satisfied.

The next five times he ordered pizza from this same place, the delivery person delivered the pizza and left without accepting any money. This is an extreme example and I am not saying you have to start giving away your inventory to satisfy an upset customer, but it does provide an example of how an upset customer does not have to be a customer lost. In general, use you own judgment and do what you can to satisfy every customer.

People rarely succeed unless they have fun in what they are doing.

Dale Carnegie

A FUNNY THING HAPPENED AT WORK –

WE HAD FUN!

A few nights ago, I was looking over some of my own training materials in preparation for an upcoming event, and something jumped out at me. One of the keys to being a successful salesperson is allowing yourself to have fun while you are selling. So today, I would like to take this time to remind you that successful salespeople are often the ones having the most fun.

I think anyone is going to do a better job at whatever they do if it is fun, but I firmly believe that it is even more pronounced in the field of sales. We work in an environment where our successes are not always as frequent as we would like. Sometimes it seems that hearing the words, "No, thank you" far outweighs hearing "I'll take it." That is when we need to remember to have fun.

The easiest and most productive way to have fun is with your customers. This is especially true if you are selling a product that is purchased for emotion, leisure or a product that is celebrated after it is purchased, (i.e. a car, a house or some form of entertainment equipment.) Selling a big, gorgeous diamond to someone celebrating a major anniversary, for example, should be fun. It is safe to assume that the receiver of the diamond is going to be excited about the purchase. This is a time where you, as the professional salesperson, need to have fun and share in your customer's celebration.

Most of us at one time or another have been a part of a sales team and even though there is still competition with your team, does not mean you cannot enjoy working with them. Play games with each other to motivate one another. Say it is a rainy Monday morning and everyone is a bit down. Go to your co-workers and suggest that whoever has the highest amount of sales today has no-cleaning duties. You have accomplished two things. One you have provided some motivation for the day. Second and more importantly, you have found a way to have fun, increase your sales, and maybe be treated to a night with no cleaning duties! Life is short. When you love your work – work becomes fun. HAVE SOME FUN!

*Profits in business come from repeat customers,
customers that boast about your product or
service, and that bring friends with them.*

W. Edwards Deming

Who's Your Buddy?

We have spent hours and hours talking about the importance of customer service and how that should be the foundation of every sale that you make. We have not talked however, about the importance of customer service after the sale. I believe that when most people hear the words customer service, they automatically think of the service that occurs during the actual sale.

Most salespeople provide quality customer service during the sale because the satisfaction is immediate and it is a means to an end. In other words, good customer service leads directly to a sale. However, the top salespeople are not on top because they make one sale to each customer. They are on top because they make multiple sales to repeat customers. So, what sets them apart from others? The difference is that the professional salespeople are providing that same high level of customer service after the sale as well. I know that people want to buy from their friend in the industry.

My automobile guy is my automobile guy because he is my buddy in the business. We do not socialize very often; in fact, we rarely see each other. However, he is my guy. Since he is my guy, he has also sold cars to my sons, daughter, and friends of mine who are in need of a car. I just happen to mention his name and give out his business card. My insurance guy is my insurance guy not because we are friends but because he is the nephew of my wife's best friend. For this reason alone, we have our homeowners insurance, car insurance, business insurance, and health insurance with him. I imagine you can guess with whom my children have their insurance. You're right, my insurance guy. I might also add that once these two people had secured my business they have lived up to my high expectations, which in turn has caused me to give them a tremendous amount of referral business.

Your business is no different, get your customers to think of you as their friend in the industry and you will be amazed at the snowball effect it will have on your productivity. Some of the things that need doing should be obvious to you including follow-up calls and written thank you notes. Many more things that need doing are usually overlooked and in the coming weeks I will share with you some of these techniques.

I absolutely believe that people, unless coached,
never reach their full potential.

Bob Nardelli, CEO Home Depot

Coaching Part One

No matter how good a salesperson is or how long they've been in the field, at one point or another, everyone is going to need help of some kind. A better word for help is coaching. As a sales manager, it is up to you to decide when coaching is necessary and how it should be completed. Each individual salesperson is different; hence the way you go about coaching them is going to be different. In short, some respond well to a "kick in the pants" and others respond better to a "pat on the back." However, some things are universal when it comes to coaching.

Coaching must always take place in a private setting and it must be set up in a way to help each salesperson specifically. It is important that you address the areas where each salesperson needs help, and come up with a plan specifically to assist them in achieving their goals. These sessions should be at a regularly set time, i.e. every Friday, and last between ten and fifteen minutes. These one-on-one sessions also allow the salesperson to give their feedback and ask questions in a private setting. It is often the lack of these types of forums that lead to bickering and rumors that eventually will undermine the staff, as well as management.

Coaching must take place consistently, and with every member of your team. Even the best players in the NFL receive coaching on a daily basis. Coaching consistently allows you to accurately track the progress towards goals, both the individual salesperson's and the company's goals as a whole. Every one of your salespeople has unique strengths and weaknesses. Only by coaching can you enhance the strengths and improve the weaknesses. The most effective way for a sales manager to be a great coach is to schedule a weekly one-on-one coaching session with each individual as close to the end of the tracking period as possible. It doesn't do anyone any good to wait a week to provide feedback. The more immediate the feedback, the more effective it will be.

Coaching is not always about pointing out the areas that are in need for improvement. It is often more effective when used to point out what each individual is doing well. Consistently acknowledge the positive; the easier it is to coach the areas for improvement.

A major benefit of coaching is having someone who helps you see your strengths and weaknesses and uses them to accomplish your goals.

Minneapolis Star-Tribune

Coaching Part Two!

We began talking about coaching and how important it is both for each individual salesperson and for the company. We will continue looking at specific things that go into effective coaching.

As we have mentioned before, we often think of coaching or training as something that is provided when someone or something needs improvement. On the contrary, effective coaching should always involve positive feedback. There is nothing more frustrating than our accomplishments being ignored. While not all people fall into this category, most of us respond better to praise than to criticism. When people leave a position, it is often because their accomplishments go unnoticed. Let's make sure we are not losing people just because we take their efforts for granted.

Every salesperson has areas that need improvement. No matter how long they've been selling, improvement is always possible. It is vital, if you want to see improvement, to not overburden a salesperson with too many areas at once. Therefore, pick one area needed for improvement. Address that specific need, and then move onto the next area.

When selecting an area for targeted improvement, start with something that directly affects the overall productivity of that person. For instance, if your salesperson is having a hard time adding-on, then addresses add-ons. Improving add-ons will increase the add-on percentage, average sale, total sales, sales per hour, and sales to goal. If you were to just address average sale, you may not improve the other numbers as well. This is why it is imperative that you know each member of your team and his or her strengths and weaknesses.

In order to achieve the best results of your coaching, you must coach the actions and not the results. It is not helping a salesperson if you say, "You need to sell more." The salesperson probably knows that he/she needs to sell more. What they need from you is coaching on how to sell more. The most effective way to make any change is to do it in increments. Therefore, we should coach to make small improvements. If you establish a goal for one of your salespeople to increasing their closing ratio by 10%, then you should coach them to increase it by 1-2 % every month. At the same time, a good sales manager will catch their salespeople doing things right and take notice.

When coaching for improvement with each individual, always use company averages for comparison. You never want to compare one salesperson to another for a variety of reasons. First, everyone is different; more experienced salespeople are probably going to achieve better numbers then those new to the field. Secondly, comparing salespeople to one another only promotes dissension and may result in decreased sales across the board. If every salesperson improves at a rate consistent with the goals you set for each of them, then the company will be successful.

Coaching is an action, not a title and actions result in success.

Byron and Catherine Pulsifer

Coaching Part Three!

We've spent a great deal of time talking about how important coaching is and some of the techniques to improve your salespeople. However, if you don't write it down, it never happened. Every coaching session you have with your salespeople has to be documented with the date and what areas were addressed. This is mainly to hold sales managers accountable. If a salesperson is not improving at an acceptable rate and there is no documentation of the coaching from the manager, then who is at fault? Any smart business owner is going to go to the sales manager first. If they are unable to provide documentation, then chances are that's whom the owner/manager is going to hold accountable. Documentation is also vital if you ever get to the point of having to terminate someone.

Any coaching is best when it is direct and concise; in other words, don't beat around the bush. If you have something to say, say it. Coaching should be done in a constructive and positive manner and those receiving the message will appreciate your honesty. Do not give mixed messages to your salesperson. During your scheduled coaching session, tell them how well they are doing in specific areas and address areas that need improvement. Provide the instruction in a concise and constructive way and move on. This eliminates any chance of the salesperson receiving a message that is different from the one you intended.

The best tool that you have when it comes to coaching is your eyes. The numbers will provide you with most of the information that you need to provide the appropriate coaching, but your presence on the sales floor will provide you with the rest. There is no better way to coach someone than by bringing up specific examples of things observed on the floor with your own eyes. The ability to discuss real life situations of what the salesperson did right or wrong is much more effective than teaching from theory or a book. Effective coaching involves teaching from both the salesperson's reality, as well as that of the company's. Even the very best can improve on something every day. It is up to the sales manager to ensure that improvement is taking place.

Wisdom is a reward for a lifetime of listening-
when you would have preferred to talk.

D.J. Kauffman

What Are They Listening To?

The other night I was shopping at a new mall here in Colorado, and I went into numerous major clothing stores. With each of these stores I visited I became more and more disgruntled with the service, or lack of service, that was or wasn't provided. In the stores I visited not one of the salespeople (a term I use very loosely for these people) approached me, asked me a question, welcomed me, offered any service, or tried to sell me anything. In each of these stores all of the employees or salespeople were wearing a headset, the question is: who are they listening or talking to? It certainly isn't the customer!

There was a time when, as a customer service, salespeople were encouraged to wear the headsets as a means to increase the level of service given to customers. The headsets were used to get merchandise, call for assistance, answer questions, call for price checks, and in general help customers to buy. I wonder if the entire concept has backfired! Now it seems that the headsets are an excuse to ignore customers. Are the people talking to their boyfriend or girlfriend? Are they catching up on gossip? Are they making prom plans, listening to the latest music CDs, or worst of all are they not listening to anything and simply pretending?

Nobody in today's world can afford to have salespeople ignoring customers. Maybe these big box national chains don't feel the effect as soon, or as directly, as the independent retailers. However, history tells us that eventually they will feel the effect. Aren't these types of scenarios the reason that the independent can still flourish? Maybe you can't match the price or the depth of inventory, but you can certainly offer exceptional service. As a salesperson in an independently owned, or customer service, sales driven organization the most important thing that any of us should be listening to is the voice of the customer. The customer wants to be welcomed, they want suggestions, they want to be shown coordinating styles, they want to be thanked and they are screaming for service. It all begins with listening and talking to customers!

*If you do not change direction, you may end up
where you are heading.*

Lao Tzu

CHANGE!

Before you all go into a full-fledged panic attack, relax. Change in life and in sales is unavoidable. When you think about it, you have two choices. You can either fight the change, or embrace it and grow with it. If we can begin to embrace it, then the goals we set for ourselves will be more obtainable. I am not here to give you a Psych 101 course on how to deal with change, but I am here to tell you that change in the field of sales is never ending, and those who learn to roll with change will be the ones reaping the benefits.

In order to continually adapt to changes, we must be willing to change ourselves. It could be our presentation, it could be a closing technique, or it could be a hundred of other things. With the economy and retail the way it is today, we cannot just sit back and wait for things to happen. We need to proactively promote our business and cause things to happen. A few weeks ago, I mentioned several ways that salespeople could drive traffic into the store. Have you embraced the change and done something to cause more people to come in? Are you looking at every sales opportunity as a chance to make a friend or life-long customer that will shop with you many times in the future? Are you asking two or three add-on questions with every retail and repair customer in order to maximize the opportunity? Are you doing a little self-evaluation after every opportunity to determine what you could have done in order to increase the quality and the quantity of the sale, or why you did not make the sale? Have you started turning over customers that you cannot close? If you are a sales manager, are you listening in on presentations and giving your people the help that they need?

The moral to this week's note is the only thing constant in the field of sales is change, and those who use it to their advantage will be the ones who remain at the top of their field. There is no doubt that change can be a little scary; but if you, the professional salesperson, can learn to love change, then you will be rewarded with success.

Respect and Trust are two way streets.

- My Father

TRUST

We talk all the time about the key to success of any salesperson in any field, which is repeat business and referrals. Certainly many things go into establishing both repeat customers and referrals. The one thing I want to focus on today is probably the most important but a lot of time overlooked as well. That one thing is simply, Trust!

Just about any salesperson can sell to one person one time. What happens when what you sold to them is not what you said it was? Do you think that person is coming back to you? Do you think they are telling their friends to go see you? They are probably telling their friends to stay away from you. I realize that all of this information is not new but I wanted to share with you a story that brought this back to the forefront of my mind.

A friend of mine and his wife refinanced their house a couple of years ago and were generally happy with the outcome. The person who helped them seemed to bend over backwards for them, and it appeared that he had helped them when no one else could. Fast-forward two years and imagine their surprise when they learn that they are in an adjustable mortgage and their payment is going up $400.00 a month.

They were never told that this was an adjustable rate loan or that this was possible two years down the road. My friends will be the first ones to tell you that they were naïve and uninformed but that does not excuse the apparent deceit that went on here. This person was not anxious to help my friends, nor was he bending over backwards for them. He was putting them in any loan that would work; at least it appears that way now. They put a lot of trust into someone who is supposed to know more than they do, and is supposed to help them find the best situation that fits their needs.

The product you are selling, the presentations you use to sell them, and your ability to get to know your customers are all very important. However, none of them mean a thing if you have not established a level of trust with your customers

A customer is the most important visitor on our premises; he is not dependent on us. We are dependent on him. He is not an interruption in our work. He is the purpose of it. He is not an outsider in our business. He is part of it. We are not doing him a favor by serving him. He is doing us a favor by giving us an opportunity to do so.

Mahatma Gandhi

All Customers Are Equal

As professional salespeople, we all understand that the people who buy from us are the sole reason that we are able to continue to do what we love. We do not get to pick our customers or choose which ones we want to sell to and which ones we do not to sell to. Every person who comes to see us is a prospective customer for life and they all deserve our best effort.

I recently went into a computer store to buy some new software for both home and the office. While I know a fair amount about computers, I knew I would need some professional assistance in order to meet my needs. I entered the store, began to look at some of the basic things I knew I would need, and patiently waited for someone to help me. I was the only one in the store but as a salesperson myself, I understand that just because a salesperson is not with a customer, that does not always mean they are not busy. They could be finishing paperwork on a sale or something of that nature.

As I continued to look around, another customer walked into the store and I noticed that the salesperson immediately approached him and began to assist him. This really bothered me, why did that customer deserve immediate attention while I apparently did not? I watched as the customer got exactly what he needed and wondered was it because he was wearing a suit and tie unlike me who was wearing jeans and a t-shirt.

I don't know what the reason was, but it did bring to mind a fundamental that a salesperson should never lose sight of -- no one customer is more important than the other. There's that great scene in the movie Pretty Woman where they would not help her because of the way she is dressed. Little did they know that she probably had more money and was more willing to buy than anyone else who entered that store that day. The professional salesperson's goal should be to help each and every customer who comes to them, while meeting their wants and needs. That means all customers deserve your professionalism in a timely manner. Remember, the customer who is wearing jeans and a t-shirt may be the biggest sale of your life. Treat them that way!

If winning isn't important, why do they keep score?

Vince Lombardi

TRACKING

Success in any field can be a fleeting thing, especially if one takes it for granted. When things are going well, the natural tendency is to ride the wave of success and ask questions later. However, when things start to go wrong, that is when we start to make adjustments or look at what we can do differently. I am here today to encourage you to take a more proactive approach as a salesperson. Tracking your store or your results, whether they are good or bad, is vital to your continued success in this field.

There are numerous ways that you could define tracking, but in this case, it is fairly simple. It involves constantly looking at what works and what does not, and the best way to go about changing what does not. Let us say for example that you are selling product A faster than your store can stock it but you could not sell product B for anything. The natural response would be to just sell more of product A to make up for the lack of sales involving product B. What happens, then, when for whatever reason product A stops selling? Now you have two products you cannot move but now product C is selling like crazy. The problem now is that you have to sell product C three times more because A and B are just sitting there. We could go on but you get the point. The bottom line is a professional salesperson will take the time and put forth the effort to find out why certain products sell and why others do not.

Are they not selling because of placement in the store, is your approach any different from product to product or is your approach too much alike? Maybe you like product A more than B and that comes through in your presentation. You may not even know you are doing it, but that is why tracking is so vital, to discover these types of things that could be hurting your sales. Some other things you can track include busiest times of the day, time of day the most sales occur, type of products people are buying and common objections to any given product.

This type of tracking allows you to continue to keep doing what is working and the ability and to change what is not. Tracking is an underused tool by many salespeople; make sure you are one who is taking advantage of every tool possible.

He who asks a question is a fool for five minutes;
he who does not ask a question is a fool forever.

Chinese Proverb

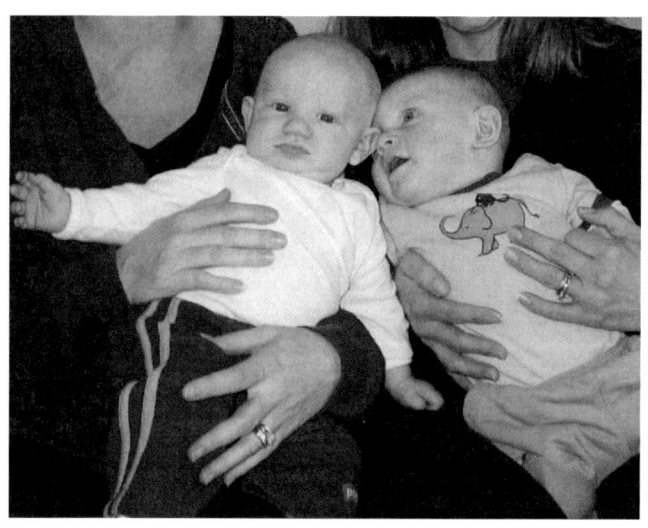

Asking Questions

Last time we discussed customer service, and how important it is to maintain a high level of customer service, even after the holidays. We discussed an example of how the ball was dropped in this one particular case; however, today I would like to keep it much more positive. The following experience happened to me while I was shopping on December 23rd at 9:30 at night.

As I am sure you can imagine, I had put off some of my shopping to the last minute and frankly was a little frantic at that point. I knew kind of what I wanted for my grandson but not exactly, and I had a ton of questions. My grandson wanted a certain type of video game and this was my objective. I do not know anything about video games, but I had the name and the system, how hard could it be? That, as it turns out, was a loaded question.

Turns out that this particular game has three different versions and only the right version will work on certain systems. Now even though I know what kind of system my grandson has, apparently there are different models of the same system. If it had not been for the professionalism of the salesperson, I may still be standing in that store looking at games. He took the time to find out primarily what game I was looking for. After quickly learning that I did not know a game system from a DVD player, he proceeded to ask me questions. As I answered his questions, he began to narrow down what type of system my grandson had, and which version of the game he would need. In the end, I bought the right game and my grandson was very happy on Christmas Day.

There are a couple of points to be made here. First, the salesperson took the time to help me get what I needed. I am sure he had been there a long time and was ready for the day and the season to end. His customer service, though, was of the highest quality. Secondly, he asked questions that he knew would lead to the answers he needed in order to find out what I needed. He may have only sold one game that night, but he also got a customer for life.

A memory is what is left when something happens
and does not completely unhappen.

Edward de Bono

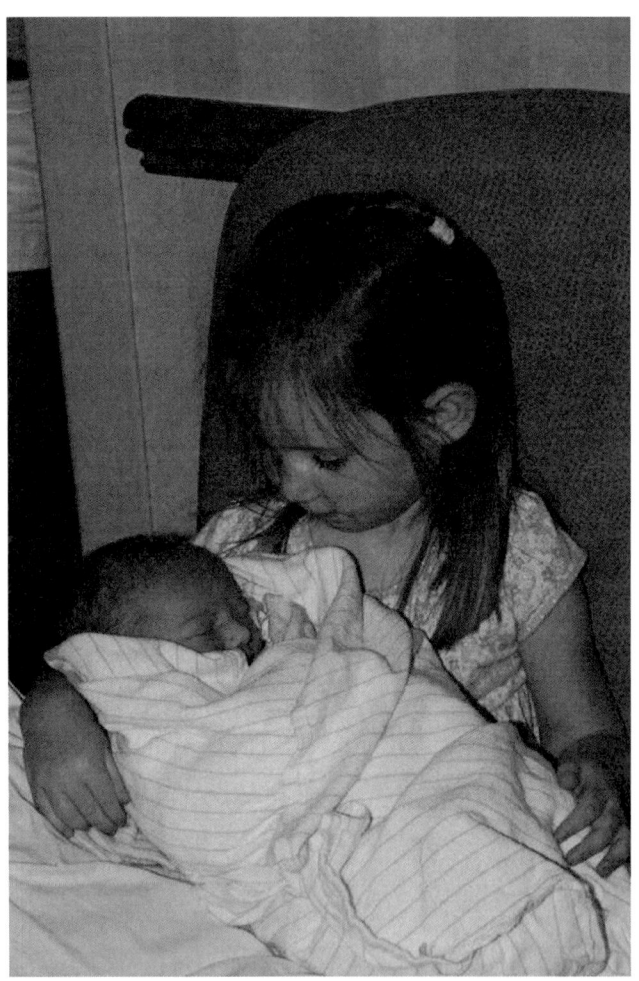

THERE IS NO EXPIRATION DATE ON

MEMORIES

I read this in a magazine ad the other day, an ad for a Visa/MasterCard, I believe. The ad showed people on vacation. This, I'm sure, was the reason for the statement "There Is No Expiration Date on Memories". I kept thinking about that "There Is No Expiration Date on Memories" and the more I thought about it the more I realized that it is so true! Not just true about vacation memories but about ALL memories. Even the memory a customer has of your store, your product, and mostly your service. There is no expiration date on a good experience or a bad one. This is why it is so important to create the best experience possible thus creating a good "memory" that lasts.

How does a salesperson create this good experience or memory? With EXCELLENT SERVICE! Service that starts with the first smile and goes on for the entire time the customer is in your store. Does it stop there? NEVER! It should go on year after year after year. You should *always* maintain a *service* relationship with your customer. How do you do that?

Try these customer service standards:

> 1) If you say it, Do it
> 2) Satisfy every customer
> 3) Keep your personal problems out of business
> 4) Use their name
> 5) Dress for success
> 6) Give them your full attention
> 7) Never interrupt
> 8) No fast talking
> 9) Sell with enthusiasm
> 10) Smile, smile, smile
> 11) Follow the golden rule
> 12) Make it fun
> 13) Go the extra mile

For a further explanation of these Customer Service points refer to pages 31 through 45 of I'm A Salesman, Not A Ph.D

Quality in a service or product is not what you put into it; it is what the customer gets out of it.

Peter Drucker

Cross Gender Selling!

I would guess that you don't need me to tell you that men and women are different. However, they are! Women and men buy for different reasons, shop differently and thus need to be treated differently during a sales presentation. Just for example, I know that the only time a man will go shopping for a new suit is when they have a special event happening within 48 hours or they blew the seat out of the suit pants that they already have. On the other hand, women may go shopping for clothing at any time. I know these are generalizations, but for the most part they are true.

When a man is making a sales presentation to women, the women may not be completely honest with the man. The same is true when a woman is making a sales presentation to a man. Should the woman be a career woman, who is a single mother, raising her children and supporting the household, what is the likelihood that she is going to tell a man that she can't afford a particular item? The chance is pretty slim. In this example, she may be more likely to tell a woman that she can't afford the item. The same is true when a woman is making a sales presentation to a man. Should the man have an ego, and some do, the likelihood of the man telling a women that she is demonstrating a product way out of his price range is rare.

When these situations occur, the man or women will probably just say to the other gender that they need to look around, this is the first place shopped, or that they will be back. When in reality, the true objection was to the price. I have previously said that when a customer gives an objection, 60% of the time the objection is not true. I believe that in a cross gender situation as much as 75% of the 60% the true objection has something to do with the price.

Therefore the answer is to handle the price objection as discussed in previous sales insights or turn the sale over to someone of the same gender. Men and women are different!

America's best buy is a telephone call to the right man.
Ilka Chase

The Unused Sales Tool!

Too often salespeople ignore one of the most valuable sales tools that they have at their disposable. The sales tool is the telephone. When used properly the telephone can generate incredible sales volume. Through proper use of the telephone a salesperson can generate both sales and added traffic for the company.

Granted there are two problems with using the telephone. One problem is the customers don't want to be called and the other problem is that salespeople rarely want to call customers. Customers don't want to be pestered by even more telephone calls than they are already receiving from numerous solicitors in various different industries. Further, salespeople don't want to be the root of the pestering and don't want to be perceived as being pushy and aggressive. I agree, I don't want to pester customers and I don't want to be pestered by solicitors.

However, I will go to the grave believing that customers want a friend in the business. Customers want someone who will give them extraordinary customer service and that has a real desire to be above average and go the extra mile. Customers want to know when new items come in, they want to know when it is time for service, and they want to know when you are having special events and promotions. I like when the room service operator calls to make sure everything was OK with my room service. I like when the service manager at the auto dealership calls to be sure all the repairs or work done on my car was completed correctly. Your customer will appreciate the effort as well.

The success of any telephone sales process starts in getting the customer to request that the salesperson call them. Once a customer has requested a telephone call the customer is much more receptive to the telephone call and you, as a salesperson, are more comfortable in making the call. The telephone is a valuable sales tool. Think about it!

One who gains strength by overcoming obstacles possesses the only strength which can overcome adversity.

Albert Schweitzer

Adversity!

Today I want to talk about the word adversity. We all face it at one time or another in our lives but it is our reaction to adversity that ultimately defines us. We all have experienced personal adversity whether it is a death in the family, a divorce, or a financial hardship. Unfortunately, we probably all have experience in dealing with adversity and have learned processes of which to overcome it. Adversity as a salesperson is going to happen as well and your ability to handle adversity will define you as a salesperson.

We are all very much aware of the financial times that we are living in and how tough things are all over. Maybe nowhere else is that hitting harder than in the field of sales; people are saving more and spending less. Which leads to obvious adversity to those who make their living selling goods or services to those people who are struggling, so how do we counteract these circumstances?

There are probably many answers, but a couple obvious ones come to mind. The first, is simply what we have always talked about, providing incredible customer service. Think about it. If you have fewer customers, then the ones you do have should be receiving a level of customer service never attained before. If a customer, during these times, comes to you to purchase whatever it is you are selling, don't you think they deserve your best efforts? Not to mention that there is a dual benefit, not only will you possibly make a sale during these tough economic times but you will probably have a repeat customer in the future. If you took the time and provided an extremely high level of customer service during tough times, then the likelihood of that customer returning during better times is probably extremely good.

Some of the other things you can do are to simply be prepared. Do not get caught sleeping, when a customer does come in, you have to be prepared. Stay on top of the details just as if you always have and always assume that the next customer is going to buy and is walking in RIGHT NOW! There is an old saying, "Tough times don't last, but tough people do!" So do tough salespeople!

*"Watch your thoughts; they become
words"*
*"Watch your words; they become
actions"*
*"Watch your actions; they become
habits"*
*"Watch your habits; they become
character"*
Watch your character; it becomes your destiny"

Unknown

There Is No Dress Rehearsal!

In sales we don't have the luxury of many other professions. There are no "Mulligans" when it comes to sales. We don't get the opportunity to do the presentation over again. We cannot wipe the slate clean and start all over again. There is no dress rehearsal. Each and every customer that we deal with is an opening night live performance in front of a New York Times critic.

In our chosen profession, every opportunity could constitute the difference between success and failure, between profit and loss, or of a sales increase or a sales decrease. Yet, many times I have to believe that many salespeople have the attitude that if I don't get this one, there will always be another potential customer coming in the door momentarily and I will sell that one. While that may be true, the one that got away makes all the difference in the world. In difficult times where the economy is suffering and customers aren't breaking down the doors to buy our products and services, this is especially true.

Now is the time for action, certainly not inactivity. Are you asking the customers all the right questions? Are you showing additional goods? Are you creating value in your presentation? Are you establishing trust? Are you selling yourself and your store or company with every customer? Are you working on handling objections and uncovering the true reason why the customer is resisting? Are you asking every customer to buy? Are you turning over any sale that you cannot complete? Are you making the experience of buying from you something that will stand out above the average? Are you sincerely greeting customers, thanking them and inviting them to come back again? Are you delivering exceptional customer service with every opportunity?

There is no dress rehearsal in sales. Every customer counts on the scoreboard. Give every customer your very best effort.

When you serve the customer better, there's always a return on your investment.

Kara Parlin

Customer Service Never Stops

We talk all of the time about customer service and how it is the most important aspect of any salesperson. In a society where customers can get virtually the same product from a thousand different stores, it is customer service that often sets one store apart from the other. Why am I telling you something that you obviously all ready know? It is simple; I had an experience the other day that shocked me, but it is also sad to say that it probably happens all too often.

I went into a local video store to rent some movies for the weekend. It was late and I got there about ten minutes before they closed. As I walked through the door, I heard employees groan and just got some awful looks. Apparently, they were not happy that they were going to have to deal with a customer in the last few minutes of their shift. As I walked through the store looking for movies, I could feel the employees looking at me as if to say hurry up. Not one of them offered any assistance and upon checking out, there was zero conversation except when they told me what my total was. There was not a thank you or a have a good night as I walked out the door. It was a dreadful display of customer service and had it not been for the fact that my family was ready to watch a movie or two, I would have left without renting a thing.

The bottom line is that customer service standards should be followed whenever there is a customer in the store, not just at the salesperson's convenience. Why is a customer who comes in right before closing should is treated any differently than a customer who came in at two in the afternoon? It is understandable that as the night winds down and you begin to get ready to close, you get anxious to go home but business hours are posted for a reason. If you are open, then please be prepared to provide quality customer service until the doors are locked.

Tough times don't last, tough people do.

Gregory Peck

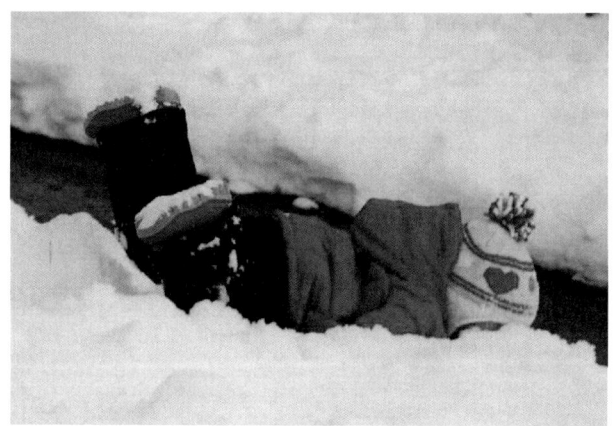

Tough Day = Tough Salesperson

I was recently talking with a friend of mine and he was telling me how rotten of a day he had and how nothing went right. He shared with me that he did not make one sale on that day and how two sales that he thought he had made fell through. In short, he just had a day that we all have from time to time.

We all have those days when no one says, "I'll take it" and you hear more objections in one day than you have heard in the previous six months. Every salesperson will have these days, but the professional salesperson will view those days as a blip on the radar screen and move on to the next day. One of football coaches favorite clichés is, "The last play is over, forget about it and move on to the next play." It's a cliché for a reason--it's true. As anyone who has been in the sales game longer than five minutes knows, there will be those days that my friend described to me but it is the salesperson who moves on to the next play that will continually find success.

The important thing to remember is not to let the bad day spill over into the next day and the day after that. We have discussed in the past about preparing for each day when you arrive at work and how that step is so vital to your success. Part of preparing for the day at hand is forgetting the previous day, live in the moment as they say. Whether you sold zero or five cars yesterday, today is a new day and the customer you are selling to today does not care what kind of day you had yesterday. If you have carried over the negative feelings that you had because of your bad day yesterday, then chances are good that those feelings will work their way into your presentation today and your customer is going to share those feelings and likely give you another no. However, if you have left yesterday behind and approached today with a positive outlook, then you are more likely to hear that customer say, "I'll take it!"

In conclusion, don't let one bad day become a bad week. Each day presents new and exciting opportunities; make sure you are in the proper frame of mind to take advantage of what every day may have in store.

No one ever attains very eminent success by simply doing what is required of him; it is the amount and excellence of what is over and above the required that determines the greatness of ultimate distinction.

Charles Francis Adams

What An Experience!

As many of you know from my tape programs or seminars, I have had a car salesman that I have dealt exclusively with for the past fifteen years. Recently this person received a promotion at the dealership, thus I was left without a car salesman that I really felt comfortable with. Luckily, I found another salesperson at a leasing company that absolutely did a fabulous job that I thought I would share with you.

Being on the road so much I have very little time to actually go out and do any automobile shopping. Therefore I called upon a leasing agent to help in the search for a new car for my wife and me. The person I found actually set up an appointment in my office to discuss the kind of car that we wanted. He and I filled out the necessary paperwork to get the process rolling. A couple of days later he called and said he had a car he wanted to bring over for us to look at. Well, we didn't like that car so over the next couple of days he brought several cars over for my wife and me to see. After a few test drives, we decided on one but didn't like the color. The salesperson went out and found the color, style and model we wanted at a dealership a hundred miles away. Then he went and picked up the car and delivered it to us. To our surprise when he delivered the car he notified us that he would have all the paperwork sent to him, he would go to motor vehicle to pick up our license plates, bring them to us and put them on the car. *He said it, and then he did it.* Imagine all of this without ever having to leave the office. <u>What a great experience</u>.

There is no question in my mind that I will, without hesitation, recommend this gentleman to others who are looking to lease a car. He did a terrific job and went the extra mile to make it an all around pleasant experience. Is buying from you and your company an experience? Do your customers leave wanting to tell others about the experience they had with you? Certainly something to think about!

*We are what we repeatedly do. Excellence,
therefore, is not an act but a habit.*

Aristotle

Consistent Application Is The Key!

No matter what the local economy may bring, what situations are facing the world, what the national or world economic status happens to be, it is the consistent application of good, sound business principles that will determine an individual's or a business's success or failure. Over the past several months I have read in trade journals, newspaper, online chat rooms and heard in simple conversations, people singing the blues about how tough business is and that it is impossible to have a sales and profit increase in these times of turmoil. On the other hand I can give dozens of success stories of companies and individuals whom have never had better times in producing sales and profit increases.

What is the difference between those that are singing the blues and those that are reeling in their success? While there could be many factors within an individual organization or within an individual's personal performance I believe it is the people and the companies that stick to the basics of running a successful business that will rise to the top. What are the basic principles in running a successful business?
Here are a few:
Having Non-Negotiable Selling Standards
Having Non-Negotiable Customer Service Standards
The constant and consistent pursuit of excellence within the company.
The consistent and on-going training of the staff.
Having goals set that are realistic and attainable based on trends.
Recognizing people for their individual achievements.
Making the workplace fun and exciting for the employees and customers.
Listening and reacting to the needs of the employees and customers.
Running the business based on facts (statistics) rather than opinion.
Communication internally and externally.
Delivering a consistent message to the customers.
Running a disciplined organization.
Consistent coaching (praising and encouraging) of the staff.
Creating an environment of personal growth and development.

If you aren't enjoying a sales & profit increase look inside before you start blaming outside influences. You may be surprised what you find.

It ain't about how hard ya hit. It's about how hard you can get hit and keep moving forward. How much you can take and keep moving forward. That's how winning is done. Now if you know what you're worth then go out and get what you're worth.

Rocky Balboa

Positive Reinforcement

There is little doubt that one of the main reasons we all work is to support our family and to earn the money for the things that we find enjoyable in our lives. We also work, hopefully, because we enjoy the challenges and rewards that our work provides. Similarly, while making a life for ourselves is the primary motivation for getting up every day, the "little rewards" often are what make it worthwhile when the alarm goes off at 6:00 A.M.

There is no substitute for positive reinforcement and the returns of simply saying "good job" to someone are often immeasurable. I have a niece who recently shared a story with me that I believe illustrates my point better than I could ever explain it. Since I have known her, she has had three or four different jobs but has never been able to find the "right job." Her previous positions all had the same basic story: she made decent money but was generally unappreciated or, even worse, treated very badly. As she was telling me about her current job, I noticed something different. There was happiness in her voice and a spark that I had never seen in all the years I have known her, so I asked her why was this job so different. Her response was, "I am happy and feel appreciated by my supervisors and co-workers." She proceeded to give me many examples. One situation was she had been working on a project for many weeks that presented many obstacles and problems, but in the end she got it done. As she was working on the project, her supervisor would say things like, "You are doing great" or "We really appreciate the time you are putting into this." When the job was complete, my niece received an e-mail from the owner of the company saying thank you and a gift card for her and her family at a local restaurant.

I have no idea what my niece makes but I do know that the positive reinforcement she received during that project probably meant more than the paycheck that went into the bank. The field of sales is often a tough one with many ups and downs and during those down times, it can be easy to get discouraged. A positive word of encouragement from a supervisor or a co-worker maybe the only thing necessary to make that person feel better about themselves and the job they are doing. So to all of you getting up at 6:00 every morning-GOOD JOB!

Most people are about as happy as they make up their minds to be.

Abraham Lincoln

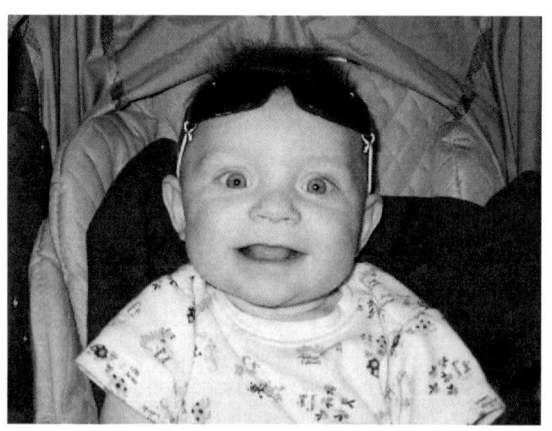

Time to Be Happy

This week I would like to take you a little bit outside of the field of sales and discuss something a little bigger. My hope is that in the end, it relates back to you and the sales field, but I think sometimes it is important to touch on something a little bigger.

I want to talk about being happy. Yes, that is what I said, happy. Too many people in this world go through life not being happy, maybe they are not sad or depressed, but they are not happy either. In all of my travels and all of the people I have met, I have learned one hard truth: if you love what you do, then chances are pretty good that you will be very good at it as well.

We talk all the time about strategies, overcoming objections, and closing techniques and while those are important, they are not what make a salesperson successful. I can teach anyone off the street how to "ask for the sale" or how to begin a non-business conversation, but does that mean he/she can sell? Of course not! Successful salespeople are successful, most of the time, because they love it and cannot imagine doing anything else. If you presented me with two young salespeople and one was very skilled in every technical aspect of sales, and the other's skills were raw, but had the love for sales, I would take the one with the love for sales everyday and twice on Sunday. Like I said before, I can teach the technical stuff but no matter how hard I try, I cannot teach the passion.

The bottom line is to find something you love and do it for a living. My hope is that what you love is sales and that is why you give me two minutes of your valuable time every week to read this newsletter. But honestly, if you don't truly love selling, then chances are you are going to be pretty unhappy.

Life is far too short to go through it not being completely happy and everyone deserves to be happy as often as possible. Someone once said, "Don't worry, be happy!" Simple, to the point, but there is a lot of truth in those four words. If you sell with a smile on your face and passion in your heart, the sales will follow. I promise!

Some girls are just born with glitter in their veins.
Paris Hilton

You Weren't Born With A Fair Certificate!

Sometimes it seems as though life just isn't fair. You don't get the breaks that others get. You are not feeling as successful as you think you should. You are not accomplishing all the things that you set out in your business life to accomplish. Other people have such an easier time learning and applying new concepts. The lucky branch seems to strike everybody except you. People you grew up with seem to have more possessions, take more vacations, work less hours and have had things given to them that you just haven't been lucky enough to get.

Success, money, accomplishments and accolades seem to come to everyone else but you. You work just as hard, if not harder, than others. You put in just as many hours if not more than everyone else, and yet nothing is ever easy for you. You have to try harder, work even more, study longer, and give more of yourself to achieve whatever it is you are working toward.

My mother-in-law used to always say that: "You weren't born with a fair certificate." I heard another person say recently that "fair" is where they give ribbons to pigs. "Fair" isn't the business world. No matter what you do, how you do it, and how much you get recognized for it, there will always be times when you feel that you weren't treated "fairly". Well, that's life!

Life isn't "fair". You have to make the breaks yourself. You may have to work harder and longer. You may have to study and read more. You also have to recognize the breaks when they do come and react accordingly. In sales you can make as much as you want to and work as hard and long as you feel. Every selling opportunity is a chance to excel and achieve success. Make the most of every opportunity and your "lucky breaks" will surely come. You are in control of your destiny.

There are no traffic jams when you go the extra mile.

Roger Staubach

A Great Customer Service Story!

My wife and I went out with family to a new restaurant a couple of weeks ago and I left there with a lesson in customer service that I would like to share with you. It's a new restaurant, and at the time it had only been open for a couple of weeks.

We were a party of five and we had just gathered on a Saturday afternoon to eat, visit, and enjoy the weather on their upstairs patio. We had been there for an hour or so and had enjoyed a couple of drinks and conversation. We ordered food and continued our conversation without much of a care when the food might arrive. Some time passed and I believed one person in our party casually mentioned how long it seemed to be taking to receive our orders. However it was a perfect Colorado afternoon and no one seemed to be bothered by the time.

Our food eventually arrived and it was all very good. The waitress later brought the check and informed us that the kitchen had gotten behind and that they were giving us some of the food for free. The waitress apologized and said that they were still working out a "few kinks." Keep in mind that not one of us complained about anything.

The new restaurant was aware of the problems and, more importantly, is aware of the fact that building a customer base is more important than the small amount of money they lost on that order. The restaurant was proactive in providing a high level of customer service without being forced into it by an irate customer. This is what high quality customer service is supposed to look like, making sure your customers are satisfied and want to return.

The customer service standards that have been set forth by this new establishment will serve them well and should be the standard that all businesses, new or old, strive to meet. Quality customer service occurs because that is the expectation, and not in reaction to an upset customer. We will definitely return to this restaurant, not only because of the great time we had, but also because of the customer service that was provided.

The moral of the story: *If you strive to provide great customer service **all of the time**, then you will reap the benefits today, tomorrow and for years to come.*

Fall seven times, stand up eight.

Japanese Proverb

The Tough Take Action!

When the going gets tough, the tough take action. No question about it, things are tough in today's economic climate. However, that is no reason to sit around and throw ourselves a pity party. Make something happen. Pull out all the stops. Approach each and every customer as if your life depended on you converting that individual shopper into a buyer. Your business life might really depend on it.

If I were running your sales floor, I wouldn't allow a customer to walk out the door unless one of three things has happened with that customer. Either they make a purchase, the salesperson captured their name, address, telephone number, or email with PERMISSION for FOLLOW-UP in the very near future, or the customer was TURNED OVER to another salesperson and that salesperson given a shot at making the sale. Every customer that walks into the store is of monumental importance. Traffic may be down over last year, but the traffic that you are getting contains more serious buyers than in the past. Our job is to convert the shopper into a buyer – nothing less.

Further, the customers that you do sell something to had better be asked to buy something else. In other words, you must attempt to add-on to every sale that is made. The easiest way to sell add-ons is to get the customer to tell you what else they may be interested in buying. Therefore, every customer had better be asked two or three add-on questions. One that I WOULD insist upon being asked is, "Who else is on your holiday gift giving list?" You know they are going to buy that other person something, it might just as well be at your store, from you, don't you think? You can save them the trouble of going from store to store, fighting the traffic, finding a parking spot etc. and heck, you will even gift-wrap it for them.

Get on the telephone; work you client lists and customer profile cards. Have gift suggestions in mind, know the customers past purchases, know their likes and dislikes – BE the expert that the customer expects you to be. Each salesperson should have a goal of making one appointment per day for each day worked, and work the phone until you make the appointment. Now is not the time to wait for customers to come in – GO GET THEM!

Put yourself in the customers place.

Orison Swett Marden

CUSTOMER SERVICE – REMINDER

I would like to take a timeout from the traditional articles and just review some important points of sales. They are just things to post and remember as you continue your work each day. I would like to start with the most important aspect of sales: Customer Service!

- **Tell the truth** – Sales and building customer relationships starts by telling the truth to your customers. Every promise you make you should keep. If you say it, do it!
- **Give the customer your full attention** – No customer is more important than the one standing in front of you. Make sure they have your complete attention.
- **Use their name** – By using their first name whenever possible, you continue to build a relationship that will build trust and lead to sales.
- **Never interrupt** – We are always trying to build relationships with our customers and one of the best ways to do that is to listen to what the customer wants. Do not forget to listen.
- **No fast-talking** – People, even in 2006, still have the image of salespeople as slick and out to stick it to every customer. Make sure you are straight with every customer and that you talk to each one as an individual.
- **Show your enthusiasm** – People who are making a purchase, big purchases in particular, are usually very excited about their purchase. Share in their excitement and do whatever you can to add to their moment.
- **Smile, smile, and smile** – It goes with showing your enthusiasm. Let the customer know there is no place you would rather be than helping them with a purchase.
- **Make it fun** – Again, buying new products is usually a fun time for your customers. Do your part to make it a good time for all involved.
- **Satisfy every customer** – Do whatever you can to try to satisfy every customer. Not everyone you meet will buy from you but try to find a way to make whatever interaction they have with you a positive one. You never know when they might be back.
- **The Golden Rule** – Last but certainly not least, treat others the way you would like to be treated and everything else will just fall into place.

You never get a second chance to make a first impression.

Oscar Wilde

The First Impression!

When a customer enters your store, or first approaches your company, they will develop a first impression. The impression that is made could be the difference between success and failure. This is especially true with new customers that haven't had an experience with you or your company. As we all know, or should know, customers are suspicious of salespeople. Through the years customers have developed a negative stereotypical perception of salespeople. Ask yourself, how many of you have had a bad experience with a pushy or overly aggressive salesperson? Then put yourself in the customers' shoes, they may perceive all salespeople as being pushy or overly aggressive.

The first impression that you make will set the tone for the entire sales presentation. The first impression may be both that you are smiling, happy, willing to serve and converse, or that you are just another stereotypical unprofessional salesperson. It is totally up to you.

Are you smiling and happy on the inside as well as on the outside? Does your body language tell the customer that you are eager and willing to serve them and their needs? Do your eyes tell the customer you are interested in helping fulfill the customer's wants and needs? Does the ambiance, or the feel of your company, make the customer feel comfortable and at "home" with your organization? Are the questions you ask designed to uncover the possible emotional aspect of the purchase? Are you focused on really listening to what the customer is saying and what might be between the lines? Is your presentation conversational or interrogational? Is the radio or sound system helping to make the customer feel comfortable with soft music that couldn't possibly offend anyone?

All these things set the tone for the presentation and the first impression that the customer may have. Look in the mirror at what the customer sees and look at your company through the customer's eyes. You may be surprised at what you see.

Some are destined to succeed, some are determined to succeed.

H.H. Swami

Destiny vs. Determination!

Few people will succeed in life because they are destined to. If you are lucky enough to be one of the destined few, congratulations! I would never fault anyone for being lucky enough to be born into success. The trick for the destined is to maintain the success and pass it on to future generations. As for the rest of us, those that will only reach our chosen levels of success through pure raw determination, keep the following thought from Paul Harvey in mind.

I wish you tough times and disappointment, hard work and happiness. To me, it's the only way to really appreciate life.

Maybe, just maybe, the times that we are now facing are a blessing in disguise. Maybe things have been a little bit too easy for the last ten to twelve years. Possibly we have gotten a bit lazy during these times of easy success. Could it be we have taken our customers a little for granted and haven't given the little something extra the makes a customer a friend? Have we neglected our ability to build on our individual strengths and challenge our own weaknesses? Maybe we haven't had to gather knowledge from outside our realm of influence, beat the bushes for leads and prospects or ask customers for referrals. Have we taken responsibility for every customer that made contact with us or have we become spoiled by our own prosperity? Maybe this little bump in the road is the best thing that could have possibly happened to us.

To me, the only way to really appreciate life and success is to have experienced both sides of the track. Life is grand; even in failure you should appreciate the experience, and turn it into another opportunity.

We see our customers as invited guests to a party, and we are the hosts. It's our job everyday to make every important aspect of the customer's experience a little bit better.

Jeff Bezos

Treat Them Like Guests!

Last week I told you about an experience I had in a car dealership with my son and daughter-in-law that started out very well and ended poorly. Let me state however, I am a believer in the statement "Every cloud has a silver lining." Today, I would like to focus on a much more positive experience that I experienced later in that car buying experience.

I am sure you can imagine, if you read the previous article, we were pretty down and frustrated with our experience earlier in the day, however, we pressed on. As we walked into the next dealership, we were met by a receptionist at the front desk and she asked, "How can we make your day just a little better?" It was not, "Can I help you?" or any other old and tired opening phrase. Considering what we had just been through, it was the perfect welcome. She then asked us if we would like to speak with a salesperson and we said yes. This next part is what really impressed me. She got on the intercom and said, "Kyle you have a GUEST at the front desk." Two things to note here, she specifically asked for one salesperson and they do not refer to their customers as customers, I am sure you noticed the word guest in capital letters. I later asked why they did those two specific things. It was explained to me by the sales manager that he does not like the image of five salespeople racing to be the first to greet a new customer (obviously Kyle was up) and that customers feel more comfortable when they are treated as a guest, rather than a customer.

We started looking at cars and talking about what we needed and that attitude filtered down to everything we did with Kyle. We were treated as guests through the entire process and all of our questions were answered honestly. Once we found a car that they both liked, we sat down with Kyle and went over the numbers. Again, we came to a payment that was agreeable to all and made our way back to financing. When we looked at the loan agreement, the payment was exactly, to the penny, what we had agreed to earlier. Treating customers like guests and keeping your promises- is a winning formula!

Never consider the possibility of failure. As long as you persist, you will be successful.

Brian Tracy

Confidence

Last time we looked at the word success and what it means to different people, and how that interacts with the field of sales. Today I would like to take a closer look at another word that is so important to salespeople: confidence. Confidence, like success, is one of those abstract concepts that is difficult to define, but has a huge impact on salespeople.

Confidence in yourself in any venture is probably the most important attribute that a person can possess. Self-confidence is often the difference between success and failure. When things are going well and it seems like you are closing every sale, your confidence seems to build and build. However, when you are struggling to close even one sale a day, then your confidence takes a hit. Those two statements are obvious, but the question is how do we maintain our confidence during those lean times?

We have all been in situations where we honestly believe no customer is ever going to say, "I'll take it" again. These are the times when you need to take a step back and remind yourself of the idea that you are a good salesperson, and then start listing examples of when you have had success. I do not care if you list those examples in your head or write them down on paper, but do a list. It will accomplish many goals but one in particular is it will force you to remember the successes, and that by itself can often change your attitude from negative to positive. If you are able to get yourself to start thinking on a positive plane again, then you can really begin to regain your confidence.

Another benefit of reminding yourself of all your successes is the thought that by thinking back, you may discover something that you were doing in the course of your presentations that you are not doing now. That one thing may be the only difference between then and now. Focusing on the things you have done well and all of the success you have had in the past will lead to the confidence you will need to be successful in the future. Every salesperson is going to go through rough patches and struggle with their confidence from time to time, but those who have the confidence to regroup and sell again will have the most success in the end. Knowledge = Confidence = Success, imagine that!

I had to make my own living and my own opportunity. But I made it.

Don't sit down and wait for opportunities to come. Get up and make them!

CJ Walker

You Gotta Love the Little Guys!

I admit I would never be labeled as someone who has a green thumb. I don't have a lot of time to work in the yard, grow a garden or to maintain the landscape of my home. As a matter of fact, I try to avoid the yard as best I can since I broke my ankle doing yard work. However, recently I decided to take on the monumental task of planting some grass seed on a few bare spots in the lawn. A simple task, you break up the soil a little bit, rake the dirt to where it is smooth, throw the grass seed down and water the area.

It all sounds so simple. As many of you know I will go out of my way to do business with the independent retailers of the world. On this day I drove an extra three miles to go to the independently owned hardware store to buy some grass seed. The big box home improvement store is about a half mile from my home and the independent if about three and half miles away. I walked into the store, went to the garden center, picked out some grass seed and started up to the cash register to pay for the purchase. At this time I was approached by a salesperson in the store to which he asked, "Do you know what you are buying?" I was a bit put off by the question but I responded, "Yes, I am buying some grass seed." To which he said, "Did you know that you picked a seed that will only grow for one season and won't grow again next year?" I had no idea that there was a difference in something as simple as grass seed. Why would anyone want to grow grass for only one year?

The salesperson guided me back to the garden center and asked what I was doing with the seed, which I responded I was filling in patches in the yard. He then directed and showed me to the proper grass seed for my needs. Do you think I would have gotten this same service and information at one of the big box stores? I don't think so! So I spent an extra few cents in gas to go the independently owned store, spent maybe 50 cents more for the product that I needed to purchase, and saved a fortune in time and effort over the long run.

Once again the little guy offers something that you can't get at many, if any, of the big box stores: Personalized Customer Service. I will continue to go out of my way to support the little guy. Think about it the next time you pull into the parking lot of the big guys!

People expect good service but few are willing to give it.

Robert Gately

Don't Bother Dave!

Last time we talked about customer service, and that we do not charge for it. We also do not get to choose when we provide excellent customer service and when it is ok to take a break. As I did last week, I have another real life example that just baffles me and still has me shaking my head.

We were shopping for some computer software and, as it turned out, it was more difficult to install than we believed it would be. Isn't it always that way? After two days of trying to figure it out ourselves, we took it back to the store where we purchased it. I spoke with the first representative who was unable to help, but did ask a co-worker who told her to call "Dave," because he would definitely know what to do. The person I was working with said she could not do that because she did not want to bother "Dave" today. Excuse me? At that point, another co-worker chimed in with this gem, "I am sorry it doesn't work but we are not bothering Dave, you will have to figure it out yourselves." You have to be kidding me, this is wrong on so many levels.

First and foremost, you have a person on your staff that you know can help a customer, who is working that day, and you don't want to bother him? That is incomprehensible to me, salespeople have jobs to provide their customers with what they want and need. This was a blatant disregard for the customer and everything that represents quality customer service.

Secondly, for a salesperson to tell a customer that they cannot help them and they will have to figure it out for themselves is unforgivable in any circumstance. As mentioned above, salespeople exist because of the customers they serve; telling them to figure it out on their own will not cut it.

We ended up taking the software to another store and they were happy to help us even though we did not buy it from them. The salesperson took five minutes and showed us how to install it. After we arrived home, we installed the software, and it worked. The store we bought it from got the sale but it will be the last, the store that provided the customer service will certainly get the rest, and I will not have to bother Dave!

Make a customer, not a sale.

Katherine Barchetti

The Bouncing Ball!

Sales are up then sales are down. One month is great the next month mediocre, and then the third month sales are down. It seems as though sales the past months have been as volatile as the stock market; bouncing up and down like a rubber ball. What is the rest of the year going to bring? I would guess a lot more of the same.

The real question becomes: are you a salesperson who is going to sit around and wait for customers to come to you, or are you going to go out and make something happen? That is really the difference between good, or even great salespeople, and those that could be labeled as exceptional salespeople. Some people, or businesses, build these ivory palaces and wait for people to come in based on location or advertising. Sometimes they don't come. "If you build it they will come," only works in the movies. In real life you have to do more than just build it. You have to give the people a reason to come to your company.

In a typical sales business there are two places to find potential customers: (1) Those that come in or contact you.
 (2) Your existing customer base.
Advertising and marketing people state that as much as eighty percent of your volume comes from twenty percent of your customer base. It seems to me the place to grow the business is in increasing the twenty percent to twenty-five or even thirty percent. In other words get your existing customer base to buy more often.

Every sales organization must have a system or methodology to maintain, develop, and maximize their existing customer base. If you don't have an extremely customer friendly, customer service driven, customer focused, clientele system, we really need to talk. You can smooth out the bumps in the road or stop the bouncing ball through proactively creating sales. The choice is yours!

Most business decisions occur over lunch and dinner than at any other time, yet no MBA courses are given on the subject.

Peter Drucker

Ask Not What Your Company…!

Ask not what your company can do for you, but rather what you can do for your company. Business in the 2000's is a give and take. For your efforts in sales you are rewarded with money and/or benefits; in return you are expected to show up on time and put in an honest day's work. You are expected to give your best effort with every customer, contribute to the team effort when it comes to non-selling duties, pull your own weight, pay for your own income with productivity, prospect, generate leads and thus generate sales.

However, too many salespeople that I encounter are waiting for something to happen. They expect the advertising to pull in thousands and thousands of people. They think the brochures, displays, signage, or general word of mouth will cause their company to become the latest hot bed of traffic, sales and profits. We all know that this isn't true; sometimes the advertising doesn't work, other times the people just walk on by without stopping, other times it is just flat dead and the phone isn't even ringing. So what is a salesperson to do? Sit and wait or make something happen?

You can certainly sit and wait, but that really doesn't sound like a good idea. I mean call me "blue boy" holding my breath waiting for something to happen, I could die before the next potential customer happens by. The other option would be to take some responsibility for yourself and make something happen for both you and your company. Heck, you might join a breakfast club, attend a chamber of commerce meeting, make a few telephone calls to existing customers or even call a few people that aren't yet customers about a new and exciting product or promotion you have coming up. You could pass out business cards at social events, talk to your friends, and stimulate some conversation at the athletic club or on the golf course. There are millions of people in this country and every one of them potentially is your customer, you just have to make the first contact.

The rewards are there for the taking. Only through self-determination, confidence, dedication and effort will the job get done. The other option is to sit around and throw your own pity party and moan and groan about how life just isn't fair. I won't be attending that party, how about you?

*Everyone is trying to accomplish something big,
not realizing that life is made up of little things.*

Frank A Clark

THE LITTLE THINGS

Have you heard the sayings, "Sweat the small stuff, and it's all small stuff." Of course you have, they have been around many years. What does that saying really mean? I suppose it means different things to everyone. I am sure there are many people that do not believe in "small stuff." I tend to agree with it for the most part, but I definitely agree with the first part of it, especially in sales.

It is easier to have a grasp on the larger aspects of sales, such as knowing prices, knowing your inventory and knowing several closing techniques. As a professional salesperson, I have no doubt that you are all experts in such things. So what separates the good from great or great from the best? It is the little things you know, the small stuff!

I was watching a baseball game the other day and it was a close, well-played game, with the win decided in the last inning. Do you know what finally won that game? It was not a homerun, a double down the line or even a well-placed bunt. It was a passed ball, the catcher just missed the ball and the runner from third scored the game winning run. The simple little thing, the small stuff, of a catcher not catching the ball lost the game for his team.

Let me give you a more workable example from the field of sales. A few months ago, a friend of mine and his wife were buying a new minivan for their family and after looking around for a few weeks, they found one that met all of their needs. During the sale, the salesperson had promised that the van would have a full tank of gas upon delivery. Now is this why my friends decided to buy this particular van, no but it was something that they remembered being promised to them. When they got in the van to drive it home, the gas tank was under half full. When they asked about the promise of a full tank of gas, my friends were told that policy ended the week before. They are very happy with the van they bought but a **little thing** promised, yet not given, left a bad taste in their mouth.

Remember, it's the little things, the small stuff, that is the difference between a satisfied customer and a repeat customer.

Customers don't expect you to be perfect.

They do expect you to fix things when they go wrong.

Donald Porter

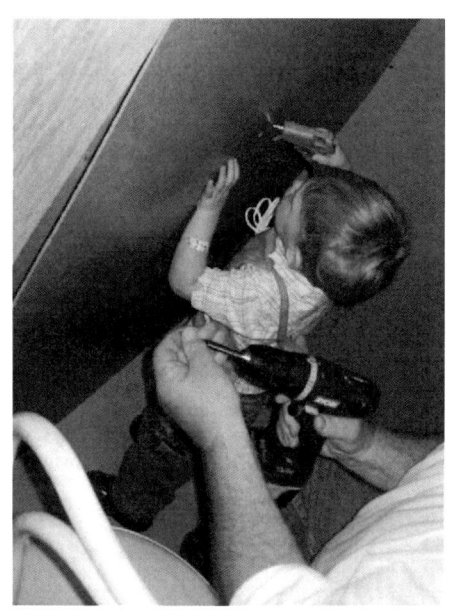

CUSTOMER SERVICE WITHOUT THE CUSTOMER

When does customer service begin and when does it end? Does it ever end or should it ever end? We can all agree that customer service is of the utmost importance when we are with the customer, but what about other times? What about when the salesperson is in the back room or talking to another employee about the customer and the customer's needs?

I had an interesting experience a few days ago which led me to ask those questions. I took my car in for repair. It had been in three weeks earlier for the same problem and they said they had fixed it, but in reality, it was never resolved. It just took me three weeks to get it back in. After speaking with the mechanic, I headed towards my favorite chair in the waiting room. After about ten minutes, I overheard a conversation that sent chills up my spine as someone who preaches the importance of customer service. The mechanic I spoke with was in the hall talking with one of his co-workers. He told his co-worker that "this guy" was in three weeks ago and they had fixed the problem, but now "this guy" is back claiming it was never really fixed. Ok, that was bad enough and you never refer to a customer as "this guy," but what followed was inexcusable. The mechanic told his co-worker that he thinks the customer (me in this case) does not know what he is doing. Had they not been making the repair free of charge, I promise you, I would have left. I almost did anyway.

Now it is obvious that the mechanic did not know I was within earshot and I hope he would not have said what he said had he known I could hear him. However, that does not excuse what happened. Not only did I hear what he said so did three other customers in the waiting room. I understand that joking around and letting off steam is a part of every profession, but we must be sure we are doing it in the right place at the right time. As long as a salesperson is at work, assisting customers, and performing work for customers, then it is vital that a high level of customer service be adhered to at all times. Remember, just because you are not talking directly to a customer does not mean they are not listening.

"Success is not the result of spontaneous combustion. You must light yourself on fire."
-Mileah Davis

Success!

What does that word mean to you? My guess is that everyone reading this right now came up with an entirely different answer. I am not nearly smart enough to come up with a universal definition for the word, but I would like to explore it briefly, and how it interacts with you and the field of selling.

When someone says, "There is the most successful salesperson in our company," what is the first thing that jumps to your mind? For me, it is that they have the most sales over a specified time. I am guessing many of you had the same thought. What if that is not what it means, what else could it mean? This very statement was said to me by a friend of mine in the business as he was referring to one of his employees and I made that mistake of assuming that he was the most successful because he had the most sales. As the conversation progressed, I learned that he was not the top seller, not even in the top five. This had me confused, so I asked my friend how this person could possibly be their best salesperson. My friend paused briefly and said because, "He is the happiest person that I know." As we talked, I learned that this salesperson sold more than enough to make a good living but he also took the time to do the things in life that he wanted to do. You do not have to work harder or longer – you have to work smarter in order to reach whatever you feel to be success for you.

If being in the top five means success to you, than go for it. I do think there is a valuable lesson in the story above. We tend to let society define success for each of us, but I think it is up to each of us to define what success is in our world.

The best summation of success that I have heard goes like this-Success lies in doing not what others consider great, but in what you consider right! Take the time to define what is right and works for you and success will follow, I promise!

Be patient and calm-for no one can catch a fish in anger.

Herbert Hoover

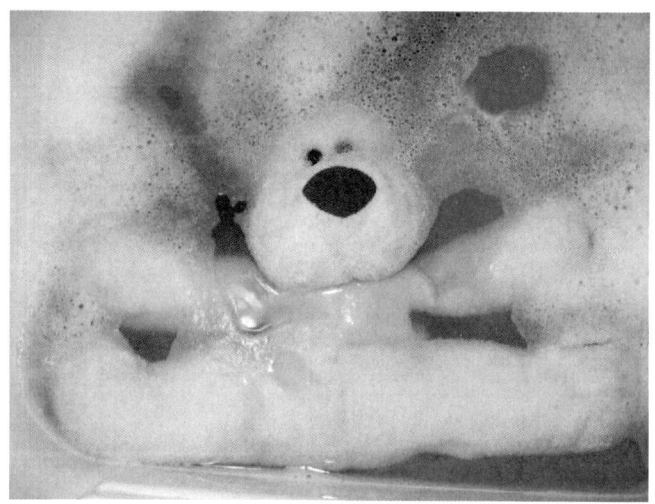

Dog Days

Welcome to the dog days everyone. In baseball, the month of August is referred to as the dog days of summer. Because that is when the season begins to drag on and on, and the playoffs are still two months away. It is the teams that fight their way through these days that often find themselves playing well into October.

The months of March and April are the dog days for many of us as salespeople. The holidays have passed, many people do not have another day off for at least a couple of months, and the weather can be pretty lousy as well. In general, there is just not a great deal for people to look forward to, and I don't know about you, but I enjoy having things on the horizon to look forward to.

The field of sales certainly is not immune to this affliction but the professional salesperson will fight their way through and find they are as successful as always. No one would argue that the toughest time to get yourself motivated to sell is the in the dull times following the holidays. That does not mean it cannot be done, however, it just takes creativity and hard work.

There are no magical formulas to selling at this or any other time of the year, but there are areas that you can focus on to help on the snowy day in March. One thing that is positive about being a little less busy is it allows you to provide more quality customer service to the people who do come in. You can carry on more meaningful conversations, you'll have time to capture name, address, phone, and email, you have time to send out thank you notes and make follow up phone calls. As we know, there is no substitute for quality customer service, spending an extra ten minutes with a customer can always be a positive thing. That time may lead to a sale and a relationship with that customer that will lead to more sales.

The main point here is simply that the time of year when traffic isn't nearly what it is in the peak months, you have the time to deliver the type of customer service that your customers want and expect. Provide exceptional customer service, implement superior sales skills and it will pay off in the end.

We cannot become what we want to be by remaining what we are.

Max DePree

The Specialist!

As salespeople, most of us have a specialty that we focus on. There are people who sell televisions who probably would struggle selling cars and vice versa. However, that does not mean one should never step outside of their comfort zone and expand his/her horizons. As we have discussed a lot recently, customer service is always the foundation of sales and increasing your quality of customer service should always be the goal.

I have noticed a disturbing trend lately, and that is salespeople who become so specialized that they are losing sight of the big picture, customer service. I recently shared with you the story of the salespeople who did not want to bother "Dave" in order to help a customer. During the same experience, I had another salesperson tell me that he could not help me because it was not his department. I asked him, "This is the electronics area, right?" His response to me was, "Yes it is but I only do games, what you have is a computer question." I asked him if he could at least point me in the right direction and he said that he had no idea who would be able to assist me. They work in the same department, not the same store, the same department.

When I went to another store to try to get an answer to my question, my faith was restored. I asked the same question to the first salesperson I came across and he said, "I don't know the answer but I know who does; let me introduce you to her." That is that way it should always be, sure we all have our specialties and areas of expertise but that should never excuse a lack of effort in assisting any customer who comes into your store.

Once again, I am not expecting a realtor to know the ins and outs of what it takes to sell computers, but I do think it is fair for a person who specializes in games to at least be able to point me in the right direction for a computer software question. In a situation like that, where it is one department you are a team and with any good team, you need to be aware of not only what you primary focus is but also the primary focus of those who work with you. The satisfaction of the customer is what is important, not what you specialize in.

"It's not what we do once in a while that shapes our lives. It's what we do consistently."

- Anthony Robbins

Consistency?

I have had the opportunity in the past several months to enjoy a terrific dinner at the same fine restaurant. What is unique about this situation is that the same fine restaurant has a few dozen locations throughout the country. Each of these fine consistent meals was at the same restaurant, however at completely different location in the country.

The waitperson gave the same introduction to the restaurant giving a brief history and story about the company and type of food that they serve. They offered the same attentive fine service from the waitperson but the assistant waiters, waitresses, bus people, host and the managers.

Further, at each of the restaurant's the main course, appetizers, side dishes and desserts all had the same fine consistency of the other restaurants I have had the opportunity to visit. The steaks were cooked the same, presented in the same manner and of the same fine quality. The cheesecake was imported from the same bakery in New York and the side dishes had the same taste and appearance.

I now know that should I be in any city in the country and look in the phone book to find a restaurant to have nice, fine meal. Should that city have the opportunity to have one of these restaurants, that's where I will be going. Simply because I now know that I will be able to enjoy the same fine experience has I have received several other times in the past.

On the other hand I have had the same lack of consistency in the meal, service, quality and experience at numerous other fast food or stereotypical chain type restaurants. In some cases it's like you are playing Russian roulette with your meals.

I wonder if your customers are receiving the same consistent fine service, product and overall experience no matter when they come in or how slow or busy you are. Building relationships and personal trade, repeat & referral customers is all about consistency at a very high level.

Great beginnings are not as important as the

way one finishes.

Dr. James Dobson

Slow Starts Don't Mean Bad Days

Fall is here and so are all of the things that go with it including: leaves turning and then falling, cooling temperatures, shorter days and of course football. If you have read this newsletter longer than five minutes, then you know the fondness that I have for the game of football. I have shared with you numerous examples over the past couple of years how football and sports in general can teach us something about the field of sales. We are now six games into the football season and there is something that I have learned that I feel can also be applied to selling.

I was watching the NFL games in week one and there were numerous surprises- some good, and some bad. Some teams with high expectations looked awful and other teams with little expectations looked great. The defending champion looked like the defending champion and looked poised to win it again. I read and listened to everyone from the media to the fans of various teams completely overreact to one game. The teams that won in week one were headed for the Super Bowl, and the teams that lost were headed for disaster.

If the teams that had lost the first game of the season had decided that the experts were right, then what would be the point of playing the next fifteen weeks? They are smart enough, though, to understand that a loss in week one is no different from a loss in week nine. In sales, do you throw in the towel for the rest of the day if your first customer that day gives you a "No thanks"? Of course, not and that is the main point here. Not every day is going to start fast or with the first sale going smoothly, but that should not dictate how the rest of the day is going to go.

Sure, we all like to start everyday with a completed sale but it is an eight-hour workday for a reason. If you did not make the first sale, what if you make the next five, all of the sudden you are five for six and having a pretty good day, right? The key is not letting a "No thanks" at the beginning of the day spill over and leading to more "No thanks" the rest of the day. Judge the success of each day at the end of the day!

Everyone is different. Sometimes it's very exciting;
sometimes very scary.

Emanuel Ax

DIFFERENT STROKES FOR DIFFERENT FOLKS

I had a recent event that allowed me to observe a couple of different salespeople work for a little more than two hours. What I witnessed was fascinating and very educational. It should be noted that my purpose for being in a position to do this was personal and it was not my intent to observe, but as I have said many times, it is an occupational hazard.

I found myself focused in on two different salespeople and because of the size of the store, I was generally able to hear most of their presentations in this two-hour period. The first salesperson, who we will call Tim, had one sales presentation that he used for every customer that he worked with. The second salesperson who we will call Bob, used a variety of different approaches with different customers.

As the day progressed, Tim did ok. He completed some sales but more often than not, he would get something like, "I'll think about it" or another such line. Bob, on the other hand, seemed to be completing sales right and left. Of course, that is a little extreme, but he was really having a good day. I continued to watch, it reinforced what I have tried to impress upon you over the years. Can you guess what that is? Every customer is different with different needs. What gets one customer to say yes may or may not get another customer to say yes. I think there is a misconception that the "sales pitch" is designed to get the customer interested in your product. I have always maintained that a professional salesperson is not selling a product; they are establishing a relationship that will lead to an optimal selling situation.

In order to achieve that, the salesperson must be willing to interact with each customer on a level that is going to gain that customer's trust and interest. Even if Tim and Bob are selling the exact same product, their customers are not buying it for the same reason. The professional salesperson needs to take the time to find out the needs and wants of each customer and then tailor their presentation to those needs and wants. We should be adjusting to the customer, they should never be asked to adjust to a salesperson.

Success is neither magical nor mysterious. Success is the natural consequence of consistently applying the basic fundamentals.

Jim Rohn

Spring Reminders

Spring is here, and for those of us who live in Colorado, not a moment too soon. I was driving around the other day and I noticed some sure signs of spring, the grass is greening up in spots, some flowers are blooming, and even some trees are beginning to bud and show signs of leaves. All of this got me to thinking about new starts and rediscovering the things that make spring, well, spring. A number of those things we tend to forget about while digging out from two feet of snow. The field of sales is the same in some ways, we work day in and day out and try to do the best we can, shoveling so to speak. However, sometimes we need reminders of the small and important things that make selling easier. Here are a few to keep in mind and revisit from time to time.

- **Use the customer's name whenever possible-** Customers, generally, like their name, so use it.
- **Non-business conversations-**Never underestimate the importance of taking the time to get to know your customers.
- **The third wheel-** Remember if a customer brings along a friend or relative, then chances are they value their opinion. Get them on your side!
- **Add-ons work-** Adding-on is an effective tool to increase your sales, and add-ons do not have to be less expensive.
- **Attitude matters-** If you are in a good mood and your attitude is a positive one, then odds are your customer's attitude will mirror yours.
- **Have fun-** Customers are more likely to buy if they are having fun and enjoying the experience.
- **Listen, Listen. Listen-** Do not assume every customer is buying the same product for the same reason. Listen to every customer's wants and needs.
- **Have passion-** If you love what you do and what you sell, then convincing others to buy it will be a lot easier.
- **Do the little things-** When everything else is equal, it is the salesperson who pays attention to the little things that will win in the end.
- **Thank you-** Take advantage of the too little used tool by salespeople-send thank you notes and/or follow-ups, they work.

Those are just ten little reminders as the flowers bloom and the weather warms up. Take this time to review some of the tools that made you the great salesperson you are today! One more thing-remember to enjoy the springtime!

Just do it!

Nike

Do More Than!

I came across the following by an "Anonymous"
author. I hope you enjoy it.

<u>Do More Than</u>

Do more than exist; Live!
Do more than hear; Listen!
Do more than agree; Cooperate!
Do more than talk; Communicate!
Do more than spend; Invest!
Do more than think; Create!
Do more than work; Excel!
Do more than share; Give!
Do more than consider; Commit!
Do more than forgive; Forget!
Do more than help; Serve!
Do more than see; Perceive!
Do more than read; Apply!
Do more than receive; Reciprocate!
Do more than advise; Help!
Do more than encourage; Inspire!
Do more than change; Improve!
Do more than reach; Stretch!
Do more than grow; Bloom! &
Do more than dream; Do!

Treat every customer as if they sign your paycheck, because they do.

Unknown

Sell To The Customer In Front Of You

The most important customer is the one standing in front of you at any given time. There are going to be those customers who will just interrupt what you are doing and start to ask you questions as if they are the only customers in the store. We understand as professional salespeople that every customer is important and we want to sell to all of them. However, you have an obligation to the customer you are currently working with to satisfy their needs and wants. After the sale is complete and the customer has left the store, then it is ok to move on to the next customer. Remember to be polite at all times and say something like, "I will be happy to help you as soon as I finish with these fine gentlemen here."

Where does all of this come from? I had an experience last week that brought this point to the surface. We purchased a new stove and had it installed last week. Apparently, our neighbors also needed a new stove and thought it was the proper time to just come on in to our house and start asking questions of the delivery people. Before I knew what was happening, one of the deliverymen was walking across the street to look at my neighbor's stove. The installation of our stove took twice as long because there was only one person working on it instead of the two that were assigned. I understand that it was rude of the neighbor to butt in, however it is up to the salesperson, in this case delivery person, to say, "I will be happy to take a look at your stove, but I am currently helping these people." That did not happen and the service we received was not nearly what it should have been.

Every customer is important, there is no question about that, but no customer is more important than the one you are currently working with. Remember to give every customer your undivided attention. Phone calls can wait, paperwork can wait, and most customers will wait if they understand why they are waiting. Chances are they will wait because they know they too will receive your undivided attention. The customer you helped yesterday is gone, the customer you will help tomorrow is not here yet, but the customer standing in front of you is ready to buy. Are you ready to sell?

Every great business is built on friendship.

JC Penny

Do You Really Know Your Customer?

Do you really know your customers? Do you know what is going on inside their heads? Are you empathetic to the wants, needs, desires and concerns of the customer? Have you put yourself in their shoes and really know what they are feeling? If you haven't, then you probably aren't as successful as you could be in sales.

Each and every customer is different. They all have different reasons for buying or not buying. The only way to maximize every potential sale is through getting to know your customers. Some customers might be buying to show love, commitment and adornment. Others may be buying to celebrate a special occasion. Still others may buy for the prestige or status along with numerous other reasons that customers buy.

The top salespeople are those that are great listeners and those that ask outstanding questions to enable the customers to express the real reason behind the purchase. In other words, take the emphasis off of the product or service that you sell and put the emphasis on the customer. A customer that is buying to celebrate a special occasion would rather talk about the special occasion than about the specific product knowledge behind the product. Share in the emotional reason behind the purchase. Then, and only then, will the customer really trust you and look at you as something other than another average salesperson.

A customer can get the same product at a number of different companies. What the customer can't get anywhere else is the service and the relationship that you can develop with them. You are the only thing that sets your company and products or services apart from all of your competition. LISTEN to your customer, and hear both what they are saying and what they are not saying, in order to maximize your potential. Additionally, fine tune the questions you ask in order to be more "customer driven" than "product driven".

Once a new technology rolls over you,

If you're part of the steamroller, you're part of the road.

Stewart Brand

Technology

In case you have not noticed, we live in a world that is much different from the one our parents live in. For that matter, the world we live in now is completely different than it was even five to ten years ago. I heard a news report recently about how fewer and fewer people are reading the newspaper these days and that the average age of a person that does read a newspaper on a daily basis is 55. The primary reason given for the decline in newspaper readership was access to the internet and twenty-four hour news channels.

In general, we live in a world now that is loaded with technology, and we, as salespeople need to know how to make it work for us. I am not naïve enough to think that you have not thought of this and not already taking advantage of the technology provided to you; however, it never hurts to be reminded.

There are so many tools out there to make your life as a professional salesperson easier and allow you to focus on your customers and meeting their needs. The first and easiest one is simply, a computer. For example, how much time have salespeople wasted in the past handwriting invoices for completed sales? I recently purchased a part for my freezer and had it installed by a professional. The person who both sold me the part and installed it had a lap top computer with a printer and upon completing the job, he was able to print out my invoice within seconds. We got to talking and he made the point to me that he is probably able to see 15-20 more people a day just due to the time he saves not having to hand write everything. Think about that, 15-20 more people a day that have the potential to say, "I'll take it."

The use of computers is probably the biggest example but there are hundreds of others. Cell phones mean we do not have to go back to the office or find a pay phone and dig for change to confirm our next appointment. Electronic date books are easier and more compact than the standard day planner is. We could go on for hours but the simple point to be made is, just make sure you are taking advantage of everything at your disposal to make yourself the best salesperson possible.

When you start viewing customers as interruptions,

You're going to have problems.

Kara Parlin

Down Time

In a perfect world, every salesperson would be busy all of the time and go from customer to customer. But we all know that we do not live in a perfect world. We all have moments, or even days, where there is a lot of down time between customers. This down time is where customer service is often compromised. The story I am going to share with you now is not directly related to sales, but it does illustrate the idea that no matter how slow business becomes, we must always be ready to provide exceptional customer service.

We ordered take-out from a local restaurant recently. It was after 8 and on a Sunday night, and I understand that business is probably a little slower during that time period. I went in to pick up our order and found myself standing in the lobby area for over five-minutes, during which time I did not see any employee, waitress/waiter or hostess. Finally someone came out from the kitchen, saw me, and called out to an employee who was bent down behind the wait station by the front door. She just never saw us or looked up at anytime. Once she saw that we were waiting, she was very professional and provided excellent customer service.

I fully understand that as a shift is ending, every employee has assigned duties to complete. It is human nature for people to want to get things done so they can go home at the earliest possible point. However customer service should ALWAYS take priority over any cleaning, restocking or other duties. Without the customers, none of those other duties are necessary.

There are still ways to complete your work and make sure that you are serving your customers. For example, the waitress who was restocking the shelves at the front of the restaurant could still do that and provide customer service. All she has to do is look up every couple of minutes, or position herself in a spot that allows her to see the front door.

No one is saying that salespeople shouldn't stay busy during down times; you can always work on closing techniques, reviewing your inventory or other such things. However it is vital that you remember that the second a customer walks in, they become your one and only priority. Remember that and you are golden!

Revolve your world around the customers

And more customers will revolve around you.

Heather Williams

The Third Wheel!

We have talked in the past about the importance of the third wheel when selling to a customer. As a quick review, a third wheel is someone who comes along with a potential customer in a buying situation. A third wheel can be a relative or a friend but it is typically someone whose opinion is valued by the potential customer. Sometimes they are just along for the ride but most of the time they are there to provide a second opinion or advice to the person looking to buy.

Because of that, we stress the importance of including that person into the selling process from beginning to end. I would like to tell you a story of how a third wheel became the customer in a big, big way.

A friend of mine was in the market for a new house and had been looking for quite a while with little success. One day he decided to take along his best friend since high school to look at new houses in the neighborhood that he wanted to buy. As my friend and the salesperson began to discuss models, the neighborhood and so on, something strange happened. The salesperson from the very start included my friend's friend in the process and as my friend became less and less interested in the house they were currently looking at, his friend, or the third wheel, was becoming more and more interested.

By the end of the day, my friend's friend, or the third wheel, had written a check for the initial down payment on his new house. My point is this, it is unlikely that this situation is going to occur very often, but by treating that third wheel like customers themselves, you are more likely to complete the sale.

When you are dealing with a customer who brings along a friend, it is important to remember that they were brought along for a reason. They obviously trust them and value their opinion. It is your job as a professional salesperson to detect that and use it to your advantage. If you can get the "friend" interested and excited about what you are saying, then chances are they will finish the job of selling whatever the product is to your customer. Then, maybe just maybe, they become a customer as well!

The only real mistake is one from which we learn nothing.

John Powell

FIVE MISTAKES TO AVOID

No matter what your field is of choice, mistakes are going to happen. There is no way to avoid them. No matter how good a wide receiver is, they are going to drop a pass here and there. Even the best writers will spell a word wrong or forget a comma. There are two certainties when it comes to mistakes- 1) They are going to happen and 2) see rule #1.

However that does not mean we should not do everything in our power to avoid mistakes, especially the big ones. Below is a list of some of the bigger mistakes to avoid.

1) **Do not talk yourself out of a sale-** We talk all the time about the importance of establishing a relationship based on trust with your customers. In order to accomplish that, the conversation must be two way.

2) **Stay close to the objective-** While we have always encouraged the use of non-business conversations to establish relationships, it is vital that you not stray too far from the objective. That objective is selling the customer what he or she wants. Avoid stories and conversations that are long and take you away from "the business at hand."

3) **Avoid technical terms-** You are a professional salesperson for a reason you are the expert. It is important for you to explain your products and/or processes to your customers in a way they can understand. Customers lose interest quickly if they feel like you are talking over their head.

4) **Have a point to your presentation-** Customers, currently, live in a five-minute world. Everyone has a ton of things going on and a million things to do. You may be number 453 on their list that day and you need to be able to grab their attention and keep it until you have completed the sale. If you are all over the place and there is no flow to what you are saying, then your customers are flowing right out the door.

5) **Ask for the sale-** Too many salespeople are so caught up in their presentation that they often forget to ask for the sale. If a customer is ready to buy and you do not allow them to say, "yes" you may end up taking back a sale you made, but never asked for.

These are just a few of the many points we could touch on however, these five represent a good starting point.

Customer service is awareness of needs, problems, fears and aspirations.

Unknown

SALESPERSON OR PROBLEM SOLVER

When people ask you what you do for a living, chances are you say "I am in sales" or "I am a salesperson." While that is certainly true, you are so much more than that whether you are aware of it or not. You are a product expert, you are a friend, and you are an advisor and so on. The one thing that you are that might be the most important is a problem solver.

Think about it for just a minute. When people are making a purchase, particularly large purchases, problems tend to arise. Those problems could be legitimate problems or they could be problems that the customer comes up with to avoid making a decision on a purchase. Chances are if customers are comfortable enough to tell you what problems they are having or what the reasons are behind not wanting to say, "I'll take it," then chances are also good that they are ready to make a purchase. They just may need a little push.

That is where you, the problem solving salesperson, comes into play. It is no different from dealing with the objections that you deal with on a daily basis. Let us say for example that a customer is interested in buying a new car but at the last minute, they say that the only problem they are having is the color. Sounds minor right and it very well could be minor and easily solved by finding the same car in a more suitable color to the customer. It could also be a sign that the customer is starting to have second thoughts and it is now up to you to find the real problem and go about solving it.

This is where you need to start asking questions to get to the real problem. It may start with something like, "I can find you the same car in blue. Would that be better?" These types of questions need to be asked until either you find the real problem yourself or the customer eventually tells you what the real issue is. Once the "real" problem is out in the open, then you can go about solving it and making your customer feel more comfortable about their purchase.

The business card may say John Doe, Salesperson but that is only the initial title. In order to be that salesperson, you also have to be a dynamite problem solver.

Coming together is a beginning, staying together is a process and working together is success.

Henry Ford

SALESPEOPLE HELPING SALESPEOPLE

I was listening to a local bank president at a seminar the other day talking about leadership. This particular individual is generally regarded as the "best" in his field and very well respected by everyone. During the question and answer session he received the following question, "How do you get better?"

My ears perked up; what a fantastic question. It would be so easy to assume that he has arrived and getting better is no longer a concern for him. His answer was even better! He said that he watches and talks to other people in positions that are similar to his. The point being that even though you are successful and "tops" in your field does not mean you cannot be better. No one understands his job better than other bank presidents do and that was his point.

By the same token, no one knows the selling game better than the people who are selling for a living. Salespeople, by nature, are very competitive with one another, but competitive does not mean we cannot learn from our competition. If I am selling houses for a living and a person I know is breaking sales records right and left, then I am going to ask them questions and try to find out what they do differently than me. It does not always mean that they are a better salesperson than you are; it just means that they have discovered something that works for them and may be of value to you.

We cannot be so competitive that we cannot learn from one another. A doctor, as talented as they may be, cannot offer advice to a salesperson on how to transition from a non-business conversation to a business conversation, but your co-worker might be very good at it. Where are you going to go for a little help? Be honest with yourself, would you have any interest in these newsletters at all if I was an out of work accountant who just decided to write about sales one day? Of course not, and you should not because only one who has been in the game can truly know what the game is like. How did you get better today?

Accept the challenges so that you may feel the exhilaration of victory.

General George S. Patton

Challenge Yourself!

As many of you know I started my sales career in retail, selling shoes. I didn't realize it then but I was lucky when I was relatively new to sales. I had a great sales manager. My sales manager was one who would constantly challenge me to reach higher levels of production and achievement. I remember when I had been with this company for a number of years the sales manager asked me a question that has stuck with me. The question was:

Do you have five years of experience with this Company, or do you have one year of experience that you have relived a number of times?

No doubt this question is very thought provoking. At the time, the truth was that I had probably two years of experience that I had relived a number of times. Most of us are not in that complex of industries. For the most part, with effort, we can learn everything we need to know from a product knowledge standpoint within six months to a year. However, it takes a lifetime to learn about people and the softer side of selling. I would recommend that everyone ask himself or herself this question on a regular basis.

Look at what you are doing and how you are doing it. Is there a better way? Is there more information available that I don't know about? Could other people have experienced the same issues and found a resolution? Learning and knowledge is the cornerstone for success. The minute you stop learning, or seeking knowledge, you are for the most part dead in the water. Even if you are a top producer, if you are not constantly striving to improve, someone else will sneak up on you and knock you off the top of the hill.

I would never fault anyone for not having knowledge. I would fault someone for not striving to seek knowledge. You can't be blamed for not knowing what you don't know. You can be blamed for not looking to discover what you don't know. Knowledge separates the mediocre from the exceptional!

.

Without change there is no innovation, creativity or incentive for improvement.

Those who initiate change will have a better opportunity to manage the change that is inevitable.

William Pollard

That With Which You Measure Will Improve!

Too often owners, sales managers and salespeople manage or base decisions on opinions rather than facts. This is the difference between objectivity and subjectivity. The only way that you can react to facts, rather than potentially fiction, is to track and react to the statistics. Statistics produce the facts that are needed today to make vital decisions in all areas of business. Yet, I find that the majority of companies do not track the correct statistics or enough statistics.

For example, if a company is trending down ten percent, the first statistic you would want to look at is traffic. Do we have as many customers as we did last year? If the answer is no, then you need to put time money and effort into advertising or getting more people to sell to. If the traffic is the same or better, the next stat would be closing ratio, or are my people selling as many of the potential customers that we do have as they were previously? If the answer is "no", then time, money and effort needs to be directed toward sales training. If the closing ratio is the same or better, the next stat you want to look at is average sale, or are my people selling as much to each customer? If the answer is no then it may be that the merchandise is incorrect or the salespeople aren't adding-on. However, somewhere in the equation the answer to why sales are decreasing will be discovered, thus enabling you to react to the facts and not just guessing. The same equation is true if sales are increasing, you have to figure out exactly "why" sales are increasing so that you can do it even better and show continued sales increases.

No matter what area of your business or productivity you are trying to improve, my advice is to attach a statistic to the issue and measure the results. If you have too much dated merchandise, start tracking the sales of that merchandise. If you are not selling enough dollars in add-on sales then start tracking the statistic.

It is an amazing phenomenon that once you track a statistic it tends to show improvement. Once you put the effort to measuring effectiveness you will show improvement. Put the attention toward whatever it is that you want to improve and you will improve. You can't effectively correct that which is not measured!

Let's not forget that the little emotions are the great captains of our lives and we obey them without realizing it.

Vincent Van Gogh

Focus On The Emotional Side!

Just in case you have not noticed, we live in a world that is full of different people and different emotions. In all my years in sales there is one thing that continues to baffle me, and that is those who believe that salespeople should not share in the emotions of their profession.

I am not talking about sharing in personal problems or issues. These have no place in the selling game. Guess what, we are human beings dealings with other human beings in a people business. Emotions and feelings are going to play a part in what we do; the question is how do you handle the emotions? Do you share them or ignore them? I would suggest that you share. When a young couple buys their engagement rings, my guess is there is going to be a lot of excitement for those two individuals. It is completely natural for the person who is selling them the rings to be excited for them as well. Honestly, it would worry me if they did not feel some of the emotion that the young couple was feeling. It makes you a better salesperson when you are able to relate to your customers on that level.

We talk all the time about three of the keys in selling; repeat customers, referrals, and establishing a customer base. Do you think a couple that buys their engagement ring from a salesperson that acted as a robot and showed zero emotion is going to leave an impression on them? Of course not, but they will remember the salesperson who shared in their "moment" and was a part of the celebration. Repeat business and referrals are certain to follow in that scenario.

This is a very simple concept! You are human, your customers are human so do not be afraid to be human with one another. By sharing in your customer's emotions, feelings, and lives, you establish a bond that robots cannot feel.

Every contact we have with a customer influences whether or not they will come back. We have to be great every time or we will lose them.

Kevin Stirtz

The Few That Make A Difference!

The headline of an article in a recent issue of The Dallas Morning News stated "Many firms push training aside." The first paragraph of the article stated that employee training can help retailers improve their customer service, but few companies invest the time and money necessary in those efforts.

An executive for the Unifi Network, which released the study stated, "We were really pretty stunned and amazed by the insights regarding retail." The study found that 41% of retail customers studied were satisfied which the shopping experience. Does that mean that 59% were dissatisfied with the retail experience? Not necessarily. Does that mean that the 41% were "WOWED" by the experience? Not necessarily. What it does mean to me however is that 59% of the people surveyed found that the retail experience was not an experience at all. It was a simple buy sell exchange of money for merchandise. The other 41% were simply satisfied. The retailers did not provide the type of customer service or "experience" that would cause a customer to come back and shop with that particular retailer over and over again.

The article gave three reasons why they felt customer satisfaction was so low. 1) The tight labor market has caused retailers to relax their hiring practices. 2) Busy managers don't think they have enough time to carefully train new hires 3) Many retailers are simply paying lip service to the concept of customer service.

Again many retailers are pushing training aside, where the few good retailers are focusing on very aggressive training and very aggressive retention. When the economy is strong and people are spending freely you might be able to gloss over average customer service. Today and into the future you cannot make excuses for poor or mediocre customer service and expect to be a well-positioned retailer. Are you one of the few that will flourish in the future or one of the many?

I only wish that I could find an institute that teaches people how to listen.

Business people need to listen at least as much as they talk.

Too many people fail to realize that real communication goes in both directions.

Lee Iacocca

"ER" – "AH"!

The other night my wife and I were at a restaurant with another couple. The waiter approached the table with a nice greeting and then asked "Can I start you off with a drink? Would you like a mixed drink er ice tea er ah a coke?" He went all around the table asking each of us would you like this er that er ah that. The "er ah" question has to be the most aggravating question in the world. Yet, the same habit is dominant in many salespeople.

I consistently hear salespeople asking questions like, "Is this for a special occasion er ah birthday er ah anniversary?" "Would you like to get her a bracelet er ah necklace er ah ring?" "Is this the first place you have shopped er ah have you been looking around?" "Were you looking for this er that er ah that?" Not only are these types of questions aggravating to the customer, they also are closed ended and don't allow for the customer to elaborate.

There is nothing more important in sales than getting the potential customer to speak. It is essential that you get them to tell you their wants, needs, desires, hopes and dreams. The information you, as a salesperson, can get from the customer may be the difference between selling additional items, one item, making a sale or not. I will stress again how vitally important it is to get your customer to speak and then for you to LISTEN to what the customer has to say. The customer will tell you what they want, why they want it, and clue you in on any potential add-on items. They will let you know how and when to close the sale, how to handle an objection, their anticipated budget, what they don't want, what they have had in the past etc. All you have to do is ***ask the right questions***.

The right questions are open-ended questions that can't be answered with a simple "yes" or "no". Every time you hear yourself or a fellow salesperson say "er" "ah" a closed ended question was just asked, I suggest you reword the question!

Don't try to tell the customer what they want.

If you want to be smart, be smart in the shower.

Then get out, go to work and serve the customer.

Gene Buckley

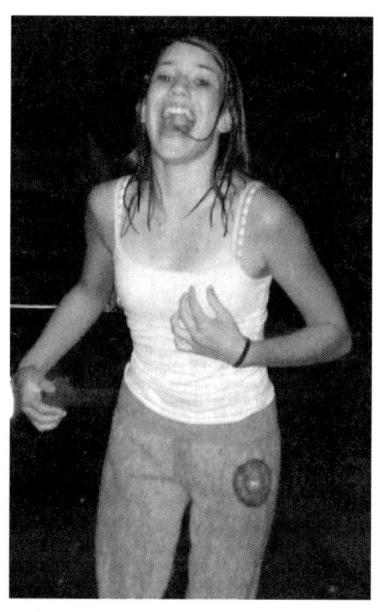

Respect the wants of your customer

We talk constantly about taking the time to get to know every customer, and the importance of finding out what they want and how to go about giving it to them. I would like to share with you two examples that happened to a friend of mine that illustrate the difference between a salesperson who does it the right way, and another who just wants to make a large sale.

My friend and his wife were in the market for a futon for their son and they went to look at them a couple of days before they were going to buy. They decided that they liked a wood model with a mattress that was fairly inexpensive. The salesperson who was helping them tried over and over to direct them over to the metal ones, which also included mattresses and were much more expensive. The salesperson never asked what the customer wanted or needed, their only objective, in my friend's eye, was to sell him the most expensive futon that he had in stock.

Two days later, when they were ready to make a purchase, they went back to the same store to buy the futon that they liked. They still had a few questions, so they found a salesperson to help them and had a completely different experience. The second salesperson asked whom the futon was for and what the age of their son was. Upon hearing that the futon was for a 12 year old boy, the salesperson recommended a wood futon with an inexpensive mattress. She said that the metal is best for people who are not going to use it for a bed very often, because the gears wear out faster if you are constantly putting it up and down. The wood futons will last much longer because it is not a mechanical system and there are fewer parts to worry about.

Obviously a substantial difference in the experience my friends encountered during the two presentations. The second salesperson took the time to find out what and who the futon was for, took the information, and sold my friends the futon that fit their wants and needs. The first salesperson only had a larger sale or bigger commissions dancing in his head. Professional salespeople make their living on repeat customers and doing the right thing for the customer. Who do you think my friend will go see when he and his wife need a bed for themselves? I think you know the answer to that one.

The biggest reason that positive endings don't happen is because employees are trained on policies and rules rather than principles.

Jeffery Gitomer

Policies Are Meant To Serve Your Customers!

For obvious reasons we spend a great deal of time in these pages discussing customer service and how best to achieve the highest possible level of customer satisfaction. We have also talked about phone customer service and the unique aspects of that. Today I would like to share with you an example of customer service by phone that left a lot to be desired.

I was recently conducting some business by phone that involved ordering some supplies and the process was fairly complicated. It required numerous phone calls and involved conversations in order to ensure that I would get what I needed. Everything was going great and I was extremely happy with the representative. We were getting close to completing the deal when I called to ask a couple of questions to check on the progress, then something happened that just should not have happened. I spoke with a representative that was not my contact and when I asked to speak with the representative that I had been dealing with for many weeks, I was told that I could not ask to speak to someone specifically. The representative told me that they could help me and they would be unable to transfer me. I shared with this person that I had been dealing with this specific representative for many weeks and they knew all of the details inside and out. I added that I would be more comfortable if I was able to complete my business with the person I had been working with from the beginning.

Once again, my request was brushed off, somewhat rudely, and I was told that anyone who answered the phone was capable of helping me. To make a long story short, I hung up, called back, and asked to speak with a supervisor. The supervisor, again, explained to me that it is company policy not to allow customers to work exclusively with one representative. However because I had been such a good customer, they would make an exception.

It is unheard of to me to deny a customer access to a salesperson that they have been working with for a specified period of time and, in my opinion, is a terrible business practice. We spend a good deal of time trying to build and foster customer relationships, let's not sabotage ourselves with ridiculous policies.

Right or wrong, the customer is always right.

Marshall Field

What If the Customer Isn't Right?

As salespeople, we often hear the phrase that, "The customer is always right." I understand the premises behind that and, for the most part, agree with the idea. There are certain situations, though, where you are going to be put in a situation where you have to tell a customer something that they do not want to hear. How do we handle that?

The easy answer is to communication with each and every customer. That's often easier said than done, especially when you are delivering good news, such as, the loan is approved, or we can accept your offer. The tough part comes when you have to tell a customer that the financing did not come through.

The first thing to remember is that 'most' people just want their salespeople to be honest with them, they may not like the news they hear but they just want to know the truth. When you find yourself in a situation where you are telling a customer something they do not want to hear, use the pointers below:

- **Be honest-** Customers can deal with a lot but will not and should not have to deal with a salesperson that is not upfront with them.

- **Be direct-** Don't beat around the bush, deliver the news in a professional manner.
- **Provide options-**Just because a customer does not get exactly what they want does not mean they still cannot be satisfied. For example, a person may be happy with an exchange rather than a full refund. As a salesperson, it is your responsibility to know and provide the options.
- **Be empathetic-** Understand that your customers may have been looking forward to this purchase for a long time and the disappointment could be great. Have understanding and empathy when delivering "bad" news.

We all prefer to be able to give the customers what they want when they want it but that is not always possible. Just remember to communicate the reasons why and be honest with every customer. If you do those two things, then most of your customers will respect you and return.

Every customer you keep is one less you need to find.

Nigel Sanders

Repeat Customers are Golden!

Over the years, we have talked repeatedly about the importance of establishing a customer base and building our repeat customer base as well. The easiest way to continue to make sales is to continue to serve those customers who have been loyal to us. However, loyalty is a two-way street and there are too many times where I see or hear about loyal, repeat customers being taken for granted. We have all done it, whether it is family, friends or customers. We take the people who are closest to us for granted and in sales that will eventually come back to haunt you.

A quick story – I knew a car salesperson who had sold a new fleet of cars for their company at the beginning of every year and he had come to count on the order to meet his goals for both January and February. For the first few years, this salesperson did a great job of staying in touch with the customer and following up on their needs throughout the year. Like clockwork, that customer would come in and purchase 6-8 cars every January. As time passed, the salesperson started doing less and less follow up and eventually just started to assume that sale every year without doing the work.

One year, the customer never showed and when the salesperson finally called to inquire why, the customer told him that the level of personal, customer service had diminished throughout the years and had finally gotten to the point where the customer felt as if their business was being taking for granted. Suddenly that salesperson was struggling to make goals and all because he assumed what had always happened would continue to happen.

Repeat customers are wonderful and that is how many salespeople make a living, so don't you think it is even more important to continue to offer the same level of service that landed them as repeat customers to begin with? We should always strive to build our customer base but we should also never lose touch with those customers who have been loyal to us. It takes so little time to make a phone call or write a note and the benefits are well worth the effort. Repeat customers are golden – do not take them for granted!

There's a place in this world for any business that takes care of its customers after the sale.

Harvey Mackay

Follow-Up – Don't Pester

You may remember that awhile back I shared with you my son's car buying experience and some of the experiences, both positive and negative that came out of that. Well as I am sure most of you know when you purchase a car or even look at buying a car, a great deal of follow up goes along with that. As a rule, follow up calls and thank you notes are always a good idea and an important part of customer service. However, as somebody once said, "Too much of a good thing is never a good idea." As before, we experienced both the good and bad of follow up and I will share both of those experiences with you.

Before they decided on the car that they ended up purchasing, they visited two or three different dealerships and looked around on the internet. (Words of advice - if you do not want to be bothered by endless phone calls then use caution when giving information to a potential seller on the web.) Anyway, for three weeks after they had visited with these dealerships they received at least two or three phone calls a day trying to sell them a car over the phone. Even after they told them that they had made their purchase and were happy with what they bought, the calls kept coming.

I am in favor of one follow up call to a customer who came in and left without buying. Maybe they have not made a decision and with all the information they received they have forgotten about their visit with you. By simply making a courtesy call, a salesperson can accomplish a couple of different things. 1) If the customer has not made their purchase yet, then maybe your call makes the difference. 2) If they have made their purchase, then you can say something like, "Congratulations, if I can be of help to you in your next car purchase, I hope you will come to see me." It is never a bad idea to keep your name and company in the forefront of a customer's mind, whether it is for now or later.

As stated in the beginning, follow up calls are always a positive piece of the selling process and you should never "pester" a customer or potential customer.

Be a yardstick of quality. Some people aren't used to an environment where excellence is expected.

Steve Jobs

Quantity vs. Quality

As salespeople, we are trained that more is better; our whole professional life has been measured by quotas, goals and charts. Obviously, the goal of any salesperson is to close as many sales as possible, but are we approaching that goal in the right way? This brings me to the point I would like to make today-quantity vs. quality. As mentioned above, we all desire quantity but in the end, the quality will determine the quantity.

Let's look at an example to help illustrate this point. If you have two salespeople who sell furniture, one is interested in how many pieces they can sell in a month and the other is interested in establishing a repeat customer base. The first salesperson comes out of the box blazing and before you know it, he has smashed his goals. The second salesperson moves steadily along and ends up having a solid month, but her numbers are nowhere near those of the first salesperson. Both salespeople have reached their goals but it certainly appears that the first salesperson came out on top. Did he?

The easy answer is yes but it is not necessarily the right answer. Keep in mind that when people go to a furniture store, quite often they are there because they have already made the decision to purchase furniture. Therefore, in my mind, it is not a huge victory to sell someone something they were already willing to buy. To me a goal is twofold; the first is obviously to close the sale on that day. The second goal is more important and often more profitable if obtained.

A professional salesperson will establish a relationship with their customer during the selling process; therefore, laying the foundation for future sales. A customer is going to be much more likely to go back to the second salesperson to purchase additional furniture because the salesperson took the time to establish the initial relationship. They are also much more likely to refer their friends/family to that salesperson for the same reasons.

The first salesperson made more sales in that one month but my bet is that the second salesperson ends up having a better year or career in the end.

Those who are blessed with the most talent don't necessarily outperform everyone else.

It's the people with follow-through who exceed.

Mary Kay Ash

Follow through to the end!

As salespeople, we know what our basic mission is and how we go about reaching the goals that we set. However, sometimes it is easy to forget that once the sale is complete, the job of a professional salesperson is not over. The tasks that I am discussing may not even be the salesperson's responsibility but it is up to the salesperson to make sure the tasks are completed or promises kept.

I have a friend who recently purchased a stove for a house that they are going to be moving into at the end of the month. Because this home is in another state, he had a friend make the purchase for him and set up all of the delivery arrangements. It turns out that his friend got the delivery date wrong, which was no big deal and should have been able to be fixed with a simple phone call.

My friend made a phone call and got the salesperson that sold him the stove. He asked to have the delivery day and location changed. The salesperson told him that he needed to contact the actual delivery company, no problem. Except that, the salesperson did not have the name of the company, the phone number and did not know how to get the information. After minutes of going back and forth, the salesperson finally got the name of the delivery company but not a phone number. My friend through his own effort finally figured it out and got everything settled but that should have never been his responsibility.

The salesperson is not directly responsible for the delivery but they are responsible for ensuring that their customer's are satisfied with the sale and including after the sale follow-up. It is inexcusable that a salesperson could not answer very basic questions about the delivery of a product. While it may not be the salesperson's fault, it is the salesperson's responsibility. In the end though, it will probably be the salesperson and the store that pays the price because the odds of a repeat customer are probably slim.

In short, just remember that your primary job is to satisfy your customer's wants and needs through the selling process. It is also your responsibility to ensure that your customers are getting everything they were promised during that sale.

When it is obvious that the goals cannot be reached,

Don't adjust the goals, adjust the action steps.

Confucius

Sometimes an Adjustment is Necessary

Today I want to look at a subject that we have examined many times before, goals. However, I want to look at them in a different context and what that context means in the field of sales.

Goals, like almost anything, are subject to change based on any number of factors ranging from the economy to the weather to life events. The main point that I want to impress on you today is that, while setting goals is important, being able to adjust them is probably more important. It is vital that the professional salesperson constantly reviews and modifies their goals to best adapt to his/her current situation.

Let's look at a real life example to better illustrate this idea. A car salesperson back in December sets a goal of selling fifty Hummers in the coming year. As we move through the winter and spring, gas prices begin to rise higher and higher. Customers that are looking to fight those high gas prices start buying smaller cars and selling fifty Hummers is suddenly no longer an obtainable goal. Does this mean the salesperson has failed because they did not achieve their goal? Of course not, the circumstances changed between the day the goal was set and now. The salesperson has no control over oil prices and the soaring cost of gas. They do have control, however, on their reaction to those circumstances. It is not a failure to not reach a set sale's goal but it may be considered a failure if one does not take the necessary steps to resolve the situation. It is a very simple process really; let's go back to our frustrated auto salesperson. It is apparent to him/her that they are not going to reach the stated goal for the reasons discussed earlier, so what does he/she do?

It is simply a matter of re-setting the goal. The salesperson reevaluates the current landscape and learns that customers are buying economy cars in order to cut their gas expense. Therefore, they lower the number of Hummers they hope to sell and increase their goals of the line of economy cars that they sell.

Goals are set as a target in achieving something but as with everything else, they should also be set with the idea that they may need to be adjusted. Set your goals and as time goes on make any necessary adjustments.

If you are not actively involved in getting what you want, you don't really want it.

Peter McWilliams

Get Involved!

I don't discuss politics in any public forum; however I thought I would use the election as a forum to encourage everyone to get involved. By getting involved I am not only talking about getting out to vote and making your voice heard, which is vitally important, but getting involved in your community as well.

Whether you are a business owner, manager or salesperson it is essential that you get involved in the community. The opportunity to network through organizations is a tremendous advantage to you and your business. Having the opportunity to shake hands and rub elbows with other people in the community can do you a world of good and give you a fabulous resource for leads and potential customers. If you are in a mall get involved in the merchant association. The mall just may tend to give more free publicity to the store and person that is active in the organization. Become involved in your church, the Chamber of Commerce, the Rotary Club, Lions Club, or in your children's parent teacher association. Become an active part of the Distributive Education program and/or the Junior Achievement Program at your local high schools, Junior Colleges and Technical Schools and Universities.

All of these avenues are fabulous resources to where you can meet and network with people in order to get more leads and potential customers. In addition, you just may have an opportunity to give back a little something to your community and the people that are your meal ticket, your customers. As an additional benefit you might just learn something as well and find some wonderful resources for finding terrific employees. I know time is a factor but if everyone in your company just gets involved with one organization the benefits will be outstanding. You will feel terrific about your contribution and the community will reward you for your time and effort.

You may not accomplish every goal you set, no one does, but what really matters is having goals and going after them wholeheartedly.

Les Brown

Reviewing Goals

We recently had a family get together and I was talking with my son and my nephew who were engaged in talk about the upcoming football season, I am not sure they ever talk about anything else. Some call them obsessed; I prefer to call them dedicated. As they were talking about training camp, it got me to thinking that this is a good time for salespeople to review, renew and revise their goals that were set for the year.

We are a little over half way through the year now and in many fields as we enter the fall months headed towards the holidays, this is where salespeople can really make some hay. So what kind of things should you be looking at or reviewing? The answer is everything but I will just take a couple of general things to give you an idea.

The first point of review is easy, are you on track with the goal you set for your personal sales? The professional salesperson set goals for a year, a month, a week, and even a day. Are you meeting those goals whatever they may be? If so, great but ask yourself are you meeting them easily and is it time to revise those goals and make them higher. If you are not meeting your goals, then you need to ask yourself why and what factors have led to that situation. If you feel as if you are working as hard as you can and are as efficient as ever, then it might be time to revise your goals to a more realistic number. However, if you think there are some things you can change that would allow you to meet your goals, do it.

The whole point of reviewing your goals half way through the year is to make adjustments. The truth be told, you should be reviewing your goals much more often than every six months but it does provide a marking point to do a more comprehensive review. The idea is not to let a disappointing first half of the year result in a disappointing year all the way around. Therefore, as you head into the fall and the holiday selling season, take an hour and examine where you in relation to your goals. If necessary, make the adjustments you need to make and ensure yourself a are Happy New Year!

Under promise

Over deliver.

Toby Bloomberg

Customer Service in Spite of the Customer

When we talk about providing high quality customer service, we automatically assume that the customer will be willing to accept our efforts. While this is usually the case, there are exceptions to the rule.

I have a friend whose refrigerator went out a few weeks ago and they began to call numerous repairmen to see if they could do anything. The first person came out and after two minutes said there was nothing he could do and that the compressor was shot. He said the compressor was under warranty, but it could take up to three weeks to get it fixed. My friend, at a loss about being without a fridge for three weeks, called the company that handles warranty repairs and they told him they could be out to look at it in a week, but only to diagnose the problem. If they diagnosed the compressor, then it could be another two weeks before they could actually get it replaced. They also claimed that while the warranty covered the compressor, it did not cover labor and anything else they may find. They talked him into spending almost $300.00 to wait a month for them to fix the fridge.

After all of this had taken place, my friend receives a call from a company he had called earlier in the day. He told the gentlemen thank you but it has been taken care of, instead of just simply hanging up, the repairmen asked if his fridge was now working. My friend, of course, said no and explained the events that had taken place before his call. The repairman said, "Ok keep that appointment for now but let me come out this afternoon, I think I can fix it today." Having nothing to lose, my friend said ok and the repairman came out and within three minutes had the fridge running again. It turned out to be a simple upgrade to provide more amps to the compressor.

Because this professional cared enough about a potential customer, he not only gained that person as a customer but he also saved my friend a lot of money and three weeks of headaches. Customers often know what they need but in some cases, your knowledge of your product or service makes you the better judge. Do not be afraid to take that extra step on occasion, it just may payoff in a big way.

*Whatever your business is, talk to your customers,
and provide them with what they want.*

It makes sense.

Robert Bowman

Roll with the Punches

Football coaches spend twenty-three hours a day thinking about every possible thing a defense could do to their offense and vice versa. Then they start thinking about the adjustments they are going to make based on what they see. Finally, once the game begins, they are still making adjustments. Half to half, quarter to quarter and play-to-play.

What does any of this have to do with the field of sales? Simple; just as the game of football is a game of adjustments, so is sales. A football coach would tell you that there is no such thing as a one size fits all game plan; they develop a plan for every team they play. In sales, no two customers are alike and the professional salesperson will learn how to adjust to meet the wants and needs of every customer.

Take for example, an automobile salesperson who is attempting to sell two cars to two different people. The first person is single, has a little money, and wants a car that represents her lifestyle. The second person is a father of three, living paycheck to paycheck, and wants a car that fits a tight budget but will carry his family comfortably. Of course the salesperson is going to show each customer different cars, but it goes beyond that. When the salesperson is talking to the first person, they are probably going to hit on things such as, fancy wheels, leather seats, and zero-60 in 4.5 seconds. When the salesperson is talking to the second person, they may highlight features like gas mileage, childproof locks, and no down payment options.

You get the point. No two customers are the same, nor looking for the same thing. If you are able to tailor your presentation to the wants and needs of your customer, then you are more likely to get both people to say, "I'll take it!" In short, have your base presentation ready at all times but do not be afraid to modify the presentation to best serve each and every customer.

People rarely succeed unless they have fun at what they are doing.

Dale Carnegie

Don't Forget The Roses

Doesn't it seem like in this day and age we are running from one thing to another and trying to do about eight tasks at one time? We are attending one kid's soccer game while we are on the phone with our spouse trying to arrange how to get our daughter from dance lessons to a friend's birthday party. Why do we do this? The simple answer is, that is life, and that's as good as answer as any. The field of sales is no different. We are running from sale to sale, closing one sale, and starting a non-business conversation with another customer at the same time. That's what we do, that's what we love to do, and I would never suggest that you don't work as hard as you can, but I will say that it's ok to slow down every now and then to enjoy what you have accomplished.

I was watching the movie Ferris Bueller's Day Off the other night, and I'm sure most of you have seen it at one point or another. I am certainly not advocating that kids start skipping school, but I think the point of the movie is an important one. The professional salesperson is good at what they do because they are well rounded both at work and away from work. It's ok to take a Friday afternoon off and go play eighteen holes of golf. It's ok to take a Monday off and take the family on a mountain getaway for the weekend. It is certainly ok for you to take a Wednesday off just to sit at home and relax. I can hear salespeople and sales managers saying, "What is he saying?" Everybody just relax. I am not saying don't work hard but I am saying that if we just take a little time to enjoy ourselves, then we are probably going to be much more productive when we are working.

Sales is what we do, it is not who we are. It is certainly an important part of who we are. The salesperson that has a balance and is comfortable with all aspects of their lives is the one that will find success. In the last scene of Ferris Bueller's Day Off, Ferris says, "Life moves pretty fast, if we don't stop and look around once and awhile we could miss it!" Don't forget to stop and smell the roses.

No man ever reached excellence in any art or profession without having passed through the slow and painful process of study and preparation.

Horace

PREPARATION

It seems to me that we spend a majority of our time discussing the actual sale or selling process and how to improve upon that. While that process is certainly the heart and soul of selling, there is a part that goes unnoticed and too often goes neglected. If neglected long enough, this part will certainly begin to affect the selling process itself in a negative manner. That part is the preparation aspect of sales, which we have hit on briefly in the past but not enough.

If you will allow me one small sports analogy, now that football season is underway. Teams have played two games already but it seems like they were just reporting to training camp. My youngest son always counts the hours until training camp opens, he understands training camps are all about preparation for the upcoming season. He is also aware that preparing does not stop after training camp is over, it is ongoing, and teams must prepare for each game.

The profession of sales is an everyday business, so I am talking about preparing for everyday and every customer. The easiest way to prepare is to prepare for everyday as it comes. For example, a car salesperson should probably prepare differently for a Saturday as opposed to a Monday. Odds are there are going to be more people who decide to shop for a car on the weekend, rather than on the first day of the work week. Therefore, the game plan needs to be adjusted. Are you prepared to discuss every car in your inventory? Are you geared up to go from the close of one sale to a non-business conversation to start another and so on? The point is not that you offer better or worse customer service based on how busy you are, because you should always give good customer service. The point is that when it is busier you need to be prepared going into the day. On a slower Monday, you may have time to prepare as you go but that may not be true on a busy Saturday.

There are so many other examples of ways to prepare for every day but you get the idea. Most salespeople stay in the field because they love what they do and are good at it, but the truly great salespeople are great because they understand that being good during the sale is because they did a good job preparing. Coaches all over the land are preparing for every possible third down play call. Are you preparing for the next objection a customer throws your way?

You never stay the same. You either get better or you get worse.

Jon Gruden

IMPROVING

Can you believe that we just celebrated the New Year and it is February already? It seems like time goes by faster and faster and yet the list of things that we want to get done grows longer and longer. The field of sales is no different in this regard. No matter what kind of year that we had last year in terms of sales, we want to be even better in 2005. There are many tools that you can utilize to ensure that this year will be better than last year. Over the next couple of weeks, we will examine a few techniques you can use to make certain that your 2005 will be a great one for you.

The first of these is time management. It seems like how we manage our time should be second nature by now, but if you are constantly seeking ways to make better use of your time, then your sales are likely to increase. Take a look over the past year and see if there were any situations where you could have either saved time or made better use of your time. For example, did you wait until the end of the day to write your estimates, quote sheets, etc? If so, then take the time to examine if writing them up at the time of the sale would have saved you time. Maybe you will find that by doing it this way, you will have an extra hour at the end of the day to make an extra sale or effectively plan the next day. One extra sale a day does not sound like a lot but twenty extra sales a month sure does. By simply changing something, as basic as the way you write up an estimate, quotes, or even thank you notes, or when, can save you time and increase your sales.

This is just one example of how a salesperson can make more use of their time but there are countless others. Take the time to examine the way you go about your day and try to pick out the areas where you think you can improve. One important note for you to remember is that time management also means finding time to relax and have some fun. If your time management skills are good, then you can be a success in sales and still be able to enjoy the football game on Sunday afternoon.

There's always room for improvement, you know it's the biggest room in the house.

Louise Heath

IMPROVING Part 2

Last week we talked about the importance of time management and how saving five minutes here and there can lead to increased sales. I would like to continue along that same line and discuss the importance of preparation. Again, this is all material that we have covered numerous times, but I think a reminder as the New Year progresses is a good idea.

Quality preparation is the key to success in any field and sales is certainly no different. I believe that we all know how to prepare on a global level, but today I would like to discuss the little things that need to be done. The first thing is preparing for each day, which sounds simple but not many people actually do it. Most people just show up for work and start working with no plan and certainly no idea of what they want to achieve that day. It is important to take five or ten minutes at the beginning of each day and decide what you would like to accomplish that day and then develop a plan to get there. You will find that it is much easier to proceed through your work if you have an idea of what it is you are trying to achieve. What customers need to be called, what orders need to be followed up on, what displays need to be reworked. A professional salesperson will develop a game plan for each workday, and then execute that plan.

It is just as important to review your plan at the end of each day. What work was done and what was not, what follow-up do I need to do tomorrow and what preparation needs to be done the following day. The end of the day is also a good time to evaluate your goals for that day and determine if adjustments need to be made. For example, if your goal was to sell 8 widgets on a given day and you sold 10, then it might be time to adjust your goal to 11 widgets for the next day. Preparation involves not only preparing for each day, but also evaluating the results of each day and then making the necessary adjustments.

Take the time to prepare and I know you will find that your sales will increase.

Change yourself and fortune will change with you.

Portugese Proverb

IMPROVING Part 3

If you listen to any great golfer, then you know that they all have one quality in common and it has nothing to do with their talent or skill. What they have is a short memory, a memory that allows them to proceed through a round of golf without getting too high or too low. The professional salesperson will adopt this principle and learn to live by it. In other words, whether or not you made the previous sale is unimportant once you have learned from it and moved on to the next sale.

Every customer deserves your best effort and demands your full attention and if you are still reliving the last sale, then chances are you are going to wind up losing two sales rather than one. By the same token, if you made the last sale and you are feeling good about what you have all ready accomplished, then you are not giving your best effort to the customer who is currently in front of you. The customer that you are currently selling to do not care that you satisfied the needs of a previous customer, they are only interested in their needs and wants being met.

A few years ago I was in the market for a new car, so I set out to find the perfect car for my family and me. The first salesperson that I worked with was very nice and acted as if they were going to help me however they could. We began looking at cars and he had a story for every car we looked at and how he sold this very car to so and so customer. That's great for him but how is a car that he sold two weeks ago to a person that I don't even know helping my needs and me? The answer is clearly not at all! I moved on to another dealership and found a salesperson that focused on what I wanted and needed in a car and together we found the best car for me.

We have all heard the sports cliché that says, "Take them one game at a time." It is a cliché because it's true and a salesperson should, "Take it one customer at a time." Your customers deserve your best effort at all times!

*There is only one corner of the universe you can
be certain of improving, and that's your own self.*

Aldous Huxley

IMPROVING Part 4

We have talked about various things to remember as we begin and continue into this year. They may appear to be little things but if tended to correctly, they can go a long way in increasing our sales. We discussed the importance of time management and how saving five minutes in the morning can lead to a sale in the afternoon. We also have discussed the importance of giving each customer your best efforts and not letting a completed sale or a not completed sale leak into your present sale. I want to conclude our little reminders for 2005 with a big reminder and it should be an obvious one.

It is vital that we remember the CUSTOMERS. Sounds like a no brainier, right? It should be and I do not believe anyone would intentionally forget about their customers and the service that we need to provide them. However, in the real world of running from meeting to meeting and the always interesting race to reach our quotas, sometimes we may lose sight of why were are in this field. As I said, none of us means to do it but it happens. This is why we need to constantly remind ourselves that our customer base is what makes those meetings necessary and those quotas reachable.

Customer service, and your ability to provide it, is the difference between you and every other salesperson out there competing with you. Thousands of salespeople are selling the same product as you, so you need to separate yourself somehow. Every salesperson provides some type of customer service to some extent. What I am talking about is going beyond what most would consider "normal" customer service. Almost every salesperson gives great customer service while the customer is in the process of buying. I am talking about things like follow up calls, thank-you notes, and the ability to establish a repeat customer base and more. We have talked about all of these things and their importance but these are the aspects of customer service that you should be reminding yourself of on a daily basis.

This is certainly not a how-to on customer service but rather a reminder of just how important it is that you are maintaining the highest possible level of customer service.

Professionalism is knowing how to do it, when to do it and doing it.

Frank Tyger

PROFESSIONALISIM

How many times over the years have we talked about non-business conversations and how important they are in the selling process? The answer is obviously a lot and I bring this up for a reason.

We have all heard the saying that too much of anything is not good for you. I had an experience the other day that I thought was a non-business conversation that turned into one very awkward experience. I was shopping for some office furniture and I began talking with a salesperson about various topics, none of which were important. It was a standard non-business conversation and I was beginning to feel comfortable with this salesperson and ready to move on to what I was looking for. That's when I first noticed a difference from almost every other experience I've ever had.

He asked if I had any kids and I said yes. Fairly standard question in a non-business conversation but I was ready to move onto the business conversation. He then asked me if they had ever really disappointed me and at this point, I am starting to feel pretty uncomfortable. I start to try and just fade away hoping to get out of this conversation but he starts telling me this story of how his son has decided not to go to college and how he and his wife had spent the past fifteen years saving for this. He went on and on about this and that and he did not know what to do. This went on for about ten minutes but you get the idea.

By now, I am sure you see what my point is, and this is an extreme example but the bottom line is twofold. One, we all have personal problems from time to time, but they can never interfere with the relationship between a salesperson and a customer. Two, non-business conversations are designed to create a level of trust between the salesperson and the customer, not to give the salesperson someone to unload on. I know that all of you reading this are far more professional than this but it serves as a reminder to make sure we maintain our professionalism at all times.

Learn the fundamentals of the game and stick to them. Band-aid remedies never last.

Unknown

FUNDAMENTALS – DON'T FORGET THEM

We have spent a great deal of time over the years discussing anything and everything that has to do with field sales and selling. We have covered everything from closing techniques to non-business conversations. All of those things, of course, are vital to the field of sales, but it seems to me that too many people continue to overlook the fundamentals.

One of those fundamentals is keeping your promises to your customers. You may be asking why I bring this up today. Well, I had an experience recently that has led me to the writing of this particular article.

I had to have some car repairs and the whole experience has left a sour taste in my mouth; but it has also served as a reminder of how important promises are to your customers. The experience started with estimates for both the cost and the time that it would take to complete the repairs. I understand that estimates are just that, estimates, but they are also designed to give the customer an idea of what to expect.

The price was higher than the original estimate, but not extremely. I do understand that cost can go up and down based on what they find as they are working. The issue that I had, and continue to have, is the time. I was initially told that the repairs would take two days to complete. Based on that information, I adjusted my schedule and started to plan ahead. As the second day ended, I was told that they would need at least two more days. While not happy, I tried to be understanding and was able to adjust my schedule. At the end of those two days, they called me and said maybe in another day or two, possibly three. At this point, I had to cancel meetings and appointments that I had made with the idea that my car would be back to me. By the end of the sixth day, I finally had my car back.

The whole experience reminded me of one fundamental idea in sales that should never be compromised. Keep your promises! Sales are about building relationships and nothing kills a relationship faster than broken promises. All the fancy selling in the world is useless without the fundamentals.

192

When you are not practicing, remember, someone somewhere is practicing, and when you meet them they will win.

Ed Macauley

Practice, Practice, Practice!

The last few weeks I have had the opportunity to work in several retail stores facilitating, observing, and coaching various role-play scenarios. In order for an adult to learn, retain and apply new information the five criteria of training must be met. To review, the five criteria of training are that the person must hear the information, read the information, write the information, role-play the information and then apply the information in real life situations.

Should any one or several of the criteria not be met, the possibility of not retaining the information is greatly enhanced. Some of us learn through reading, others learn through writing, others learn through visual means, and still others learn through hearing information. The only way that one can insure that the knowledge and information is being digested and retained is through role-playing and the actual application in real situations.

While many people resist the process of role-playing, it is the single most effective means of insuring that the information is understood and thus able to be applied. Many important aspects of a person's natural tendencies seem to come out in role-play situations. You may find that your natural tendency is to interrupt frequently. You may find that you sound somewhat interrogational rather than conversational. You may uncover that the communication delivered is totally different than the communication received. You may find that will you think you are asking quality questions of the customer, in reality the questions are closed ended and cause people to be less communicative than you had perceived.

My suggestion is that you get a partner, write out, reread and then role-play as many aspects of the selling process as possible. You may be surprised at the weaknesses and the strengths that come to light throughout the process. Role-play enough and your customers may actually start following your role-play scenarios.

Your best customers leave quite an impression.

Do the same and they won't leave at all.

SAP Ad

Image!

What image does your advertising project to your customers? What image do the salespeople project to the public? Are the images advertised the sales images delivered? Far too often in business the image that a company is trying to convey via their advertising message is totally different than the image that the business conveys in live customer to employee situations.

Many of the big box stores advertise knowledgeable, friendly and attentive sales staffs only to completely fail when it comes to the service given on the sales floor. Car dealers offer huge discounts or low monthly payments through their advertising, only to find that only one or two percent of the public would qualify for the special discounts or low interest payments. Car rental companies advertise ease in processing, only to have the customer get hung up at the rental counter due to incompetent counter people. Airlines advertise on time departure and arrival, only to find the next few flights taken are late in arriving and/or departing.

Salespeople should operate under the umbrella of being a direct and essential representative of the advertising and marketing program that a business projects. The advertising may be the first indirect impression that a potential customer has of a business but the salespeople are the first direct impression. In many cases the customer may decide to buy based on the first few minutes of contact with the salespeople. Customers will make a conscious or subconscious decision of whether they will ever return to a business based on the impression that the salespeople make with the customer. While all business generally promote a positive, customer service driven image in their advertising very few live up to the expectation when direct contact is made. The difference between a simple, nothing special buy/sell relationship and a WOW experience on the part of the customer is in the impression and image that the salesperson projects and leaves in the customer's mind. Only through living up to the image that the advertising projects, will a business grow to reach its full potential.

Always give your customer something.

Kevin Stirz

START ADDING-ON EARLY!

The entire process of adding-on can be perceived as being very pushy and aggressive. This is true not only in the customer's mind, but in the salesperson's mind as well. Yet, adding-on is a customer service. The customers may really need the items you sell. They just may not know they need it yet, or they are unaware of the wide range of different items you sell.

When I first became involved in the jewelry industry, I heard a jeweler say that pearls were a traditional gift for the groom to give to the bride. I wondered at that time if my wife was disappointed years ago when she didn't receive a wedding day gift from me. I had never heard of the tradition and didn't know it even existed. Whose fault was it that my wife didn't receive a wedding day gift? Was it my fault or the jeweler's that sold me the engagement and wedding ring? I believe that it was the jeweler's. People will never ask you for, or buy from you, something that they don't know exists or that they are supposed to be buying.

Should that jeweler have said to me somewhere in the presentation; "Oh, by the way, what did you have in mind as a wedding day gift for your bride?" I would have responded, "What? I didn't know I was supposed to be getting her a wedding day gift." At which point the jewelry salesperson could have told me that pearls were a tradition. I don't know if I would have purchased the pearls at that point, but the likelihood would have been higher after having talked about it than it was when not even mentioned.

In every selling scenario there are appropriate add-on questions. When you start asking the questions early, as part of the sales presentation, the customer will perceive it as a customer service. If you make an add-on suggestion after the fact, or after the customer has made a decision, then adding-on will be perceived as pushy and aggressive. Look at every selling scenario and develop some appropriate questions to set-up the add-on early in the selling process.

You'll never have a price or product advantage again. They can be duplicated, but a strong customer service culture can't be copied.

Jerry Fritz

It might be a little thing that goes a long way!

I just got back from filling up my car with gas, so I guess retirement will have to wait a few more years. I am not here to further depress you about the high cost of gas, or for that matter, the higher prices on everything. On the contrary, I would like to offer some ideas to help the salesperson through these difficult times.

No one is immune to the current situation and every salesperson is facing the same issues, so the question becomes where we find an edge. The answer is to focus on the little things. While it may not be feasible to lower prices at this time, it is always feasible to satisfy our customers. Just a few minutes ago when I filled my tank with gas, I had given the choice of a free soda or coffee. That is the promotion going on now at this particular station if you fill your tank. A complimentary drink does not completely erase the sting of dumping half of a C note into your car but it can go a long way in establishing a repeat customer base. When prices drop, I will remember what that station did for me and I will buy all my gas from them. This is just one example of a business doing the little things to make the lives of their customers just a tad better.

Here are a few examples that represent those little things. If a company delivers, maybe they could leave a small token of their appreciation. A car salesperson could offer five free tanks of gas with the purchase of a new car. (A couple of manufacturers are already doing something all like this.) A jeweler could offer a free dinner for two at a local restaurant with the purchase of an engagement ring.

You get the idea! Let your customers know that you understand that times are tough and you want to be there to help them through. Any salesperson can maintain good customer relationships during good times, but a salesperson willing to go the extra mile for customers during the tough times that will increase their customer base and loyalty for the good times.

It starts with respect. If you respect the customer as a human being and truly honor their right to be treated fairly and honesty, everything else is much easier.

Doug Smith

Don't Let Your Customer Down!

How many times have you told a friend that you are busy and you will call them tomorrow, but that call never occurs? Come on, be honest. We have all done it and probably done it more times than we can even remember. However, when you tell a customer that you will call them back or return their call tomorrow, you had better make sure that you follow through on that promise.

I was recently shopping for homeowner's insurance and my first phone call was to the company that carries my auto insurance. I have always been satisfied with them and their service and thought that this was the logical place to begin. I spoke with my agent and we discussed a number of options. I had a payment due on my current homeowner's policy and he said that he would get back to me within a day or two and let me know if I should make that payment, or if he could offer me a better rate. Two days passed, then five days passed and I ended up sending my payment. I must have some type of insurance, the payment was due, and not paying it may have resulted in cancellation of the policy. Another three weeks passed, and I heard nothing from my agent, so I eventually broke down and called him. Naturally, he was in a meeting, so I left a message for him to call me. I never received a call back. I called back again a couple of days later and left yet another message. He finally called me back and told me that he could not beat the rate of my current company and that is why he did not call me back to begin with.

The fact that he could not improve the rate on my homeowner's policy is not the point. He made a promise to look into some possibilities that we discussed and promised to call me back. He failed to deliver on that promise and now maybe my homeowner's insurance agent can help me with new auto insurance as well. The moral of the story is simple; if you say you are going to call a customer at a given time, then follow through. There is nothing more frustrating than waiting for a return phone call that is never going to come.

Friendly makes sales-and friendly

generates repeat business.

Jeffrey Gitomer

Remember the Customer!

As you know, my travels take me to all ends of the United States. As I make those travels, I continue to run across all kinds of people. Salespeople to be exact, and truthfully most of them do an excellent job. However, they do often provide some quality examples of what works and what does not in our field. The one thing that I have continued to notice is that customer service seems to be better when the business is smaller.

There are probably multiple reasons for it, but I believe that it comes down to one fundamental point, and that is the respect the businesses have for their customers. Smaller stores tend to have fewer customers and, therefore, treat each and every one of them as if they are their only customer. Now there is certainly nothing wrong with big stores and chain stores but there are times when the one on one touch with the customer gets lost amongst the 30 aisles of product. Having all of that product, though, does not matter if there is no one to buy it.

Smaller stores cannot compete with the larger competition strictly based on product and price. In fact, they usually have fewer selections and their prices are generally higher. Where they can compete and often beat the bigger stores is in their customer service. They rely on repeat customers and referrals but most importantly, they rely on the most important thing to any salesperson: the customer.

My point today is not to tell you that the big chain stores are not good at what they do because most of them are. My point is a lot simpler than that. **Remember the customer!** That is it, that is my point today. It does not matter how many different kinds of widgets you sell or how many salespeople you have to sell them, if there are no customers to buy them.

No matter how big or how small a business is, ultimately the customers determine the success or failure of any sales business. As long as professional salespeople remember that, then any business, big or small, will be successful. PLEASE REMEMBER THE CUSTOMER!

Learn to say thank you every time.

Jill Griffin

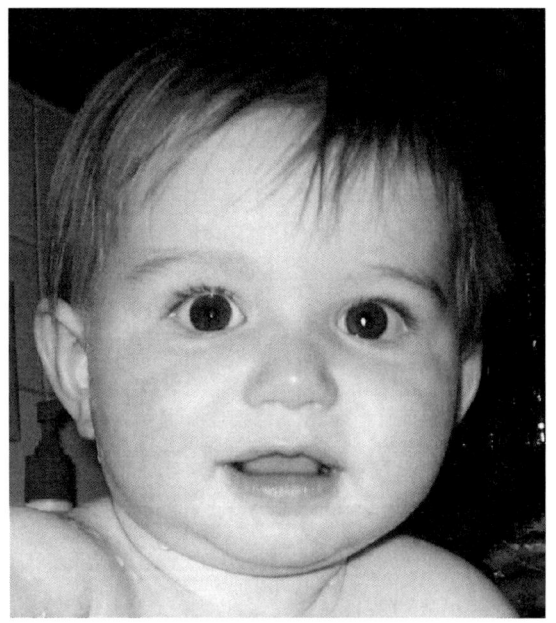

FOLLOW UP ON MISSES TOO

We have talked numerous times about the importance of follow up calls and thank you notes, and we have discussed how vital they are in order to establish referrals and repeat business. Today, I would like to talk about an experience that I recently had to illustrate that importance.

I was recently in the market for a new modem for our home computer and had narrowed down my choices to two modems. They were at two different stores, which of course had different salespeople. The modems had equal capabilities and either one would work well with the current computer in our home. In the end, though, I am no different from anyone else, I went with the modem that was less money; a penny saved is a penny earned you know.

I took my new modem home and hooked it up and everything worked fine for about a month but then it began to do odd things and eventually it quit working all together. I called the store and the salesperson that I purchased the modem from to see what my options were. They explained to me that because the modem was not an exact match to my computer, they could not do anything for me. They did give me a list of common problems and the way to fix them, the same list that came in the box by the way.

As my frustration grew and I heard more and more excuses why they could not help me, I received an unexpected lifeline from an unexpected source. The salesperson that I did not purchase the modem from was calling to thank me for coming into his store and to see if he could help me in the future. As we were talking, I told him about the problems I was experiencing with the modem that I had purchased and he began to ask me a series of questions. After three questions, he told me what the problem was and how to fix it. Sure enough, the modem worked and I have never had a problem with it since.

The first salesperson may have gotten my business once but the second salesperson will get the rest. Never underestimate the importance of follow up calls and thank you notes; sometimes they pay off even when you did not make the sale.

Treat your customer, as you would want

to be treated as a customer.

Catherien Pulsifer

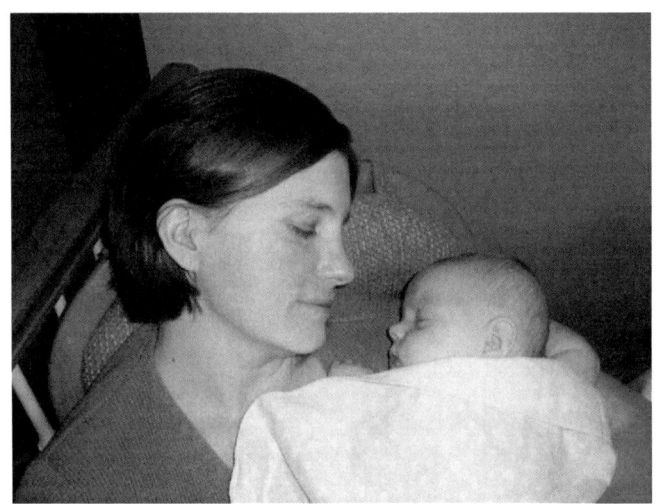

Don't Forget The Most Basic Strategy!

Sometimes we spend so much time talking about different techniques and tools that we should be using we forget the most fundamental ideas. The most basic of those ideas is simply the first lesson we ever learned in Kindergarten. The Golden Rule: treat others the way you would like to be treated.

I had an experience over a three-day period that annoyed me and I would like to share that experience with you. I was at a friend's house for a barbecue a couple of weeks back and there were a number of people there, all having a good time. There was one individual, though, who was insulting to everyone and had a negative comment for everything. Almost all parties have someone like that and I am not here to talk about someone who ruined my good time. It is the second part of the experience that is interesting.

Two days after the barbecue, my cell phone died and I went in search of a new one. I proceeded to the store that I had bought my last phone from and as I was looking around, I noticed the same obnoxious person from the party in the store. As it turns out, he is a salesperson there. He walked over to me and asked if he could help me. He was nice and professional; however I walked out of that store without saying a word or purchasing a phone. I could not believe that this was the same person who, two days earlier, was insulting various people for various reasons.

The point is simple. You are always networking, even when you are not trying to. I did not go to that party to make a contact in order to purchase a cell phone but due to a chain of events, that is where I ended up. If the salesperson had just been civil at the barbecue, when I recognized him in the store, I would have probably purchased a new phone from him. The bottom line is, you never know where your next customer is coming from, so treat others as if they might be your future.

Our attitude towards life determines

life's attitude towards us.

John N. Mitchell

It Is About Attitude!

As you can probably guess, I am usually thinking about sales and customer service and how one or both can be improved. I guess it's an occupational hazard. The difference between failure and success can boil down to the attitude that you have. Customers can feel when a salesperson enjoys what they are doing and have a great attitude. On the other hand, they can also feel when someone is having a bad day or just hates what they are doing.

I was recently in a restaurant having lunch with a friend of mine and everything was good from the service to the food. I didn't take much notice of it at the time but then my friend said something to me as we were leaving that got my attention. He said, "Isn't it nice when people who are there to help you act like they want to be there and want to make sure you are satisfied?" I started thinking about that statement and the only word that came to mind was, DUH!

I do not say that to be cute or funny, but rather as a statement of the obvious. How often do we come away with the type of feeling that my friend shared with me? I hope it is more times than not but I am guessing it is not as often as it should be. We are in sales, of course, and a big part of that is customer service but I also believe quality customer service comes from those with positive outlooks and attitudes.

If you are in the market to make a purchase and you have narrowed your choices down to two, and everything from price to warranties is identical; the only difference is between the two salespeople who helped you. One salesperson is pushy and does not really seem to care about anything but closing the deal. The other salesperson is friendly, takes an interest in you, and truly wants you to be happy. The question is this, from who is 99% of the public going to buy that item? I think you know the answer.

The point is a simple one. If you are enjoying what you are selling and the customers that you are selling to, then odds are your customers will enjoy buying from you, hopefully more than once.

As we express our gratitude, we must never forget that the highest appreciation is not to utter words, but to live by them.

John F Kennedy

Thank You Is Always a Good Idea

I recently shared with you a story about a friend of mine who purchased a new computer and phone system for his business. We discussed the importance of salespeople sometimes having to work together in order to completely satisfy the customer and their needs. Something else recently came out of that story that I also would like to share with you.

We talk a great deal about the importance of thank-you notes and follow-up calls when it is appropriate. We have discussed sending thank-you notes when a sale is completed or when a salesperson is thanking a customer for coming in and considering making a purchase from them. Those are both great reasons for a thank-you note and as we have discussed before, thank-you notes and follow-up calls continue to be an underused method of contact by many salespeople.

As I told you before my friend shopped a few different companies and spoke with different salespeople before making his decision. A few weeks after making that decision and ultimately having his new systems installed, he received a thank-you note. Very appropriate, don't you think? Especially after the business that he had just thrown the way of the company; however, there is a twist. The thank-you note was not from the company he had made his purchase from, it was from one of the companies that he had looked at but decided to buy elsewhere.

The thank-you note thanked him for coming in and giving them the chance at earning his business. It also said that while they were sorry that they did not do enough to earn his business, they will continue to be there for any for his future needs. They also offered to service the equipment he had just bought from a competitor if he became unsatisfied with the service he was currently receiving.

This particular company may not have gotten the initial business from my friend, but because of a simple thank-you note just for coming in, they will probably get a majority of his business in the future. Think about that for a minute, a company that turned a turn down into a repeat customer by taking five minutes to say thank-you. Moral to the story: never underestimate the positive effects of a simple note and/or follow up call.

*Trust is like a mirror... once it's **BROKEN** you can never look at it the same again.*

Unknown

In the Field of Sales

In the field of sales, we all understand that there are a few basics. As in any field if you do not have the basics down, then you are going to struggle to succeed. Today I want to touch on one of those basics that were completely ignored the other night, and how it should have been avoided. The basic in this case was keeping your promises.

Our family recently went out to dinner, something we do not get to do very often. Therefore, when we do get to do it, it is a big deal and we look forward to that time together. Without going into great detail, the service was not good. We sat at our table for ten minutes before getting a waiter and our food took forever to come. However, that is not the point of today's article.

The point I would like to touch on today is how the situation was handled and there were ups and downs in that respect. For the most part, it was dealt with fairly well. Both the shift leader and the manager came by to offer their apologies, and the manager said he would pay for the appetizers. That was great and we were satisfied with that solution. However, after that had been settled our order took a very long time to come out and then came out one dish at a time and some of the food was cold or undercooked.

At this point, the shift leader came over and said the entire meal would be taken care of as a gesture of good will. Again, we were satisfied with that resolution. Towards the end of our meal the manager came over and said that he was sorry but the shift leader did not have the authority to "take care of the tab" and that we would still have to pay. I do not mind paying for what I buy but a **promise** was made and I expect that promise to be honored. If the shift leader did not have the authority to do that, then you take it up with them but the customer has been **promised** a free meal for their troubles. I explained my position to the manager and eventually he agreed and the meal was free. Mistakes happen but if they are addressed and the customer leaves satisfied, then no harm done. As a professional salesperson, if you make **any promise** to a customer-keep it!

People only see what they are prepared to see.

Ralph Waldo Emerson

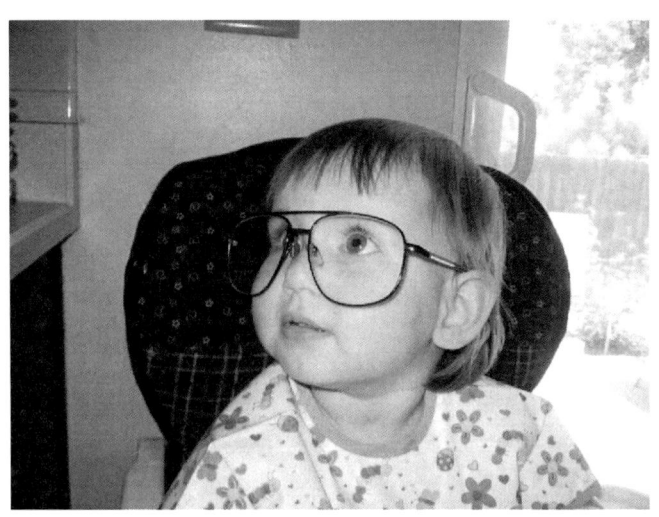

Perception Equals Reality

We have all heard the saying that perception is reality, right? I think that is true to a point and I especially think it can be very true in the field of sales. As you know, most of your encounters with your customers are brief and often a first time event. Therefore, it is even more important for salespeople to take full advantage of the time that they do get with each and every customer.

Because our time with customers is often brief, first impressions become that much more important. That is where the term perception is reality comes into play. I would like to tell you about something that I saw over the holidays, which still bothers me now. I walked into a store to find a gift for my wife. Upon walking in, I noticed three salespeople standing behind the counter talking and laughing. There were five potential customers in the store and at least two of them were obviously seeking some help. Eventually the two customers got the attention of the salespeople and I assume they got the help they needed.

I do not know for sure because I left the store without looking at a thing. Why, you ask? It is simple; my perception was that the three salespeople did not care whether I was there or not. Is that the reality? Maybe, maybe not; but that is the perception that I walked out of that store with. If, as a salesperson, you are active and acknowledge the presence of each and every customer that enters your store, the more sales you are likely to make.

Every salesperson gets busy from time to time but even if you say to a customer, "I'll be with you as soon as I am done here" then the customer is much more likely to be patient and wait for your assistance. There is never an excuse for customers to be present in the store and three salespeople not responding to any of them. Not only is that terrible customer service, but it also gives off a perception that the salespeople do not care about their job or the customers they are supposed to be serving. After awhile that perception becomes the reality and those salespeople will have all kinds of time to talk because there will not be any customers.

Make your reality one that people perceive to be great!

Our greatest asset is our customer! Treat every customer as if they are the only one!

Laurice Leitao

IF I HAVE SAID IT ONCE!

I bet I have said this a million times but I am going to say it again, PAY ATTENTION TO YOUR CUSTOMER. The last Sales Insight focused on one part of paying attention to your customer, listening to your customer. This Insight is about a different kind of attention, *acknowledgement*. You know what I mean, simple attention.

I am still amazed at how many times I am in a given establishment, which by the way boasts excellent customer service, and I can't get a salesperson to pay attention to me. To go a step further I can't even get them to take my money. Time after time I have to search to get help and when I find someone it seems as though they don't want to be bothered with me. Maybe they are aware of my identity and fear my critique and the possibility they and their establishment will be featured in my next Sales Insight, (yea, right) never the less it is sad.

This type of treatment of customers is actually quite common, unfortunately, and happens to people other than myself. Last week I was in Las Vegas for the jewelry conventions and stayed at two different hotels. My wife joined me for this trip and while I worked she "shopped". She really does not enjoy shopping nearly as much as losing money in the slot machines, but it is something that *must* be done. Besides she loves to report back to me any "non – customer service like" treatment. Well she had a full report for me and to quote her: "I walked up to the cash register to pay for some items I picked out for the grandchildren and the "cashier" (dubbed so because gift shops never have salespeople) was on the phone. Her entire duty is to take my money and she was on the phone chatting for at least five minutes while I stood there right in front of her, money in hand. She did not even bother to say she would be with me in a moment, she just ignored me!" I think you all know by now how I feel about this but I will say it anyway. Take your phone conversations off the sales floor.

That evening we went to dinner and when we walked into the restaurant the hostess says, "Two for Dinner?" then points to a table rather than taking us to it. Why didn't we just seat ourselves?

Tomorrow's battle is won during today's practice.

Samurai Maxim

POOR – OK - GOOD – GREAT or OFF THE CHARTS

The countdown has started. There is only twelve weeks to go to the big season. I was in Florida last week and some of the malls and department stores have already started putting up the holiday decorations. Are you kidding me? It is a month before Halloween. I haven't even picked out my costume yet and they are trying to sell me holiday merchandise? WOW!

This is not the point. The point is you have worked the last nine months planning for a great holiday season. You have purchased your merchandise and it is on the way. The advertising and your holiday catalog are in the final production stages, those special promotional events planned, scheduled, and the final details worked out. You had some remodeling done over the past couple of months and the place looks sharp. It is going to be a great holiday season, MAYBE.

What have you done with your most valuable asset, YOUR PEOPLE? How have you gotten them prepared? Have you given as much attention to the one thing that will really make the difference between a Poor – OK – Good – Great – or OFF the charts Holiday Season? Have you taught them how to start making appointments now for early November (when you have the best selection) with the top 25% of your customer base? Do they know how to speed up the selling process while developing relationships? Do they understand the importance of add-ons, handling objections, creating value, sharing in the emotional excitement of the purchase? Do they know to plant a seed for a future purchase, ask for referrals, capture contact information, with permission, for future follow-up, how and when to turn over a sale, how to close, recognize buying signs, and on and on? Or did you do such a great job of buying and advertising that all your customers are going to come in and say "I'll take it" and "Give me a few of those too", and "I'll see you again at Valentine's Day" because your such a great place to shop.

I would rather not risk it. I would take the next 8 weeks and TRAIN, TRAIN, TRAIN. Help your people be the best that they can be. Help them be the expert that they want to be and your customers expect them to be. The difference between Poor – OK – Good – Great – and OFF the Charts will come down to one additional sale made a day by each of your people. Knowledge is cheap – a lack of knowledge costs a fortune.

Every wall is a door.
Ralph Waldo Emerson

HITTING THE WALL!

In running, there is a term known as "Hitting the Wall". What the term means is that mentally, emotionally, and physically the runner is totally and completely drained and can't take another stride. They are simply out of gas. Each and every runner has a different point at which they hit the wall and cannot continue.

I believe the same thing is true in business as well as with individual salespeople. Every business and every salesperson will eventually "hit the wall". The business or salesperson will not be able to go any further, produce any more or reach the next level of sales and productivity. Sales will level off and complacency may even become commonplace. The business and the individual will keep doing the same tasks, selling the same way, and producing the same results.

The only cure for "hitting the wall" is first, recognizing what your "stops" are and secondly, soliciting outside intervention from experts. Learning what your "stops" are can be very difficult. It is a process through which a business or a salesperson recognizes weaknesses that are causing a lack of growth. When does the individual salesperson give up on the sale and hand the customer a business card. Telling the customer that when you are ready come back and see me. Is it that enough questions weren't asked? Was it that the salesperson couldn't handle the objection? Was it a lack of product knowledge? Is it that the business is run on opinions rather than facts? Does the sales manager/owner lack the confidence when it comes to making decisions? Does the business have a culture of personnel growth and development?

These are all questions that a business owner and individual salesperson should be asking themselves along with many others. The key to growth and further accomplishment is within you. Recognize when you "hit the wall" then acquire the knowledge to move on.

*Words should be used as tools for communication
and not as a substitute for action.*

Unknown

Say It With Feeling!

Last week we talked about the differences between men and women when it comes to buying. When it comes to selling I have also discovered some differences as well. I have recently found that women possess a far greater vocabulary when it comes to speaking in emotional terms compared to technical terms. This may not be completely true; it may simply be my own deficiency.

Selling is a process of communication in which the salesperson expresses the message in colorful, exciting, lively words to create value and desire of a product or service for the potential customer. I do know that in selling products or services the wider your vocabulary the better, especially when it comes to feeling words.

For this reason I give you the following list of emotional or feeling words that you can and should work into your presentations. These words will enable you to drive the emotional aspect of the communication and enhance the perceived value of the purchase in the customers mind.

Alive	Anxious	Delighted	Ecstatic
Elated	Cheerful	Energized	Fantastic
Amused	Glad	Fortunate	Overjoyed
Fulfilled	Thrilled	Wonderful	Proud
Pleased	Relieved	Thankful	Warm
Wonderful	Confident	Determined	Intense
Energetic	Bold	Brave	Positive
Loving	Healthy	Potent	Secure
Spirited	Solid	Active	Eager
Dismayed	Satisfied	Certain	Powerful
Aggressive	Sure	Absolutely	Intimidated
Envious	Embarrassed	Crushed	Devastated
Jealous	Fragile		

This is just a partial list and there are hundreds of other powerful words you can incorporate into your sales presentation. Think about every word and phrase that you say and determine if there may be a more powerful way to express your sales message.

The ability to learn faster than your competitors may be the only sustainable competitive advantage.

Arie de Geus quotes

Let's Step Outside For A Minute!

Let's step outside for just a few minutes. In other words, one of the best places to learn about your strengths and weaknesses is through your competition. Far too often salespeople don't see beyond the four walls that they work in for hours every week. This practice can cause a salesperson to sell with blinders on.

The customers are shopping from place to place and see all of the differences between like businesses. To not have the same information, or more, as the potential customers is simply foolish. From the outside looking in I would guess that everyone looks pretty much the same. The real differences become apparent once the door has been opened and the truth is in clear vision. Shop your competition as the customer does, with the intent to buy something. Ask questions to find out what the hot sellers are, look at the pricing structure, and see when they offer a discount. Take notice to whether the presentation is customer driven or if the salesperson is trying to sell you on why they like the product. Make note of the questions that they ask. See if they try to proactively close the sale or attempt to get your name address and phone number. Make an active effort to determine exactly what your competitive advantages are against the competition, or the competitions against your own company.

The name of the game is to stay six months to a year ahead of anything the competition is doing. If you are now the "Top Dog" in the marketplace, I assure you someone at some point will be trying to knock you to second place. I would also assure you that the competition is probably shopping you. Great business people know and understand that the business has to be in a constant state of change in order to remain on top, or to reach the top. I would also encourage you to ask the competition questions about your organization. See what they are saying about you and your company. It may be very enlightening.

There is a wealth of information available to you in the business down the street. There are hundreds if not thousands of things you can learn by keeping an eye ahead of you, behind you and next to you. Lose sight of the competition and chances are they are so far ahead you may never see them again. The lead dog by far has the best position and view. Be the lead dog by stepping outside every now and then.

*Opportunities are usually disguised as hard work,
so most people don't recognize them.*

Ann Landers

Opportunity!

Last week, we talked about the adversity that salespeople are facing in this economy and how to make the best of it. Often out of adversity comes opportunity, and that is what I would like to discuss today. Yes, we are facing difficult times but those times are not going to last forever, believe it or not. The question is, are you, the professional salesperson, going to be ready to take advantage of those opportunities when they present themselves? Yes, there may be more "down time" now than we would like but it is time to take advantage of that "down time", not wallow in it.

First, this is an excellent time to sharpen your sales and customer service skills with the customers you do have. Secondly, we talked about when you sell someone in these tough times then the likelihood of him or her becoming a repeat customer increases drastically. However, in order to take advantage of future opportunities, there are things you can be doing now.

If a store is not as busy as it usually is, this provides a good time for salespeople to get some additional training. Not even the best salespeople know everything and continuing one's learning process is always a plus. Use this time to know your product and operations. If you have fewer customers, then there should be no excuse for not knowing your product(s) inside and out. Read the manufacturers information, know the difference between different models, know what the products can, and cannot do. It may seem like tedious work now, but has huge payoff benefits when things improve, and they will improve.

The last thing I want to touch on is our attitudes. I am not going to turn into Dr. Phil on you, but I do think it is important that, as professional salespeople, we maintain our focus and positive attitude. It is easy to get down when it has been slow for two or three days. However, if you allow yourself to get down and become negative, then what happens when the next customer does walk into the door? Are you in the right frame of mind to sell or are you feeling negative?

Opportunity is always a customer away and times will improve-are you ready when they do?

228

Here's a simple but powerful rule: always give people more than what they expect to get.

Nelson Boswell

Go the Extra Distance

There are so many companies and salespeople out there in all industries and customers have more choices today than ever before. My question for today is how do we make sure we are getting our share of this ever increasingly large pie? The answer is simple, and you know what it is. It's customer service, of course. However, I am not talking about your everyday type of customer service, I am talking about customer service that goes above and beyond what most would consider a "normal level" or doing as Jack Mitchell calls hugging your customer.

I think back to the time that I bought a television on a Friday night and it was a big sports weekend, with the local team playing on Monday night. Because we lived outside of their normal delivery area, it would have been the middle of the next week before it could be delivered. The salesperson that sold us the television understood that we would like to have it over the weekend, at least in time for Monday night's game. He promised us that he would find a way to get it on a truck and out to us the following day.

We left the store a little nervous that we wouldn't be seeing our new television before Wednesday of the following week. The next day, the hours past and it got to be 5:00, still no TV, and no calls about a delivery time. At 5:15, our salesperson called and told us that he was unable to get the television on a truck but he had just gotten off work and had the TV in his own truck and was on his way to deliver it himself. Sure enough, by 5:45 he was carrying our new television into our house and even doing all the installation himself. We had our new TV not only to watch Monday night football but also to watch all the football we wanted on Sunday as well!

What I am trying to get across is this: Every salesperson in every profession performs some type of customer service but it is the *professional salesperson* that will go the extra distance to satisfy their customers who will reap the rewards of repeat and referral business. Going the extra mile does not always have to entail as much effort as delivering a television but anything that makes it easier for the customer to buy or receive the product they bought is what real customer service is all about. This type of customer service is what separates the professional salesperson from those who just work in sales.

If it's not fun, you're not doing it right.

Bob Basso

PLAY A GAME – MAKE IT FUN

No matter what profession a person is in, we all face some of the same trappings and obstacles on a day-to-day basis. I think one of the biggest things we all face at some point is just the repetitiveness of work and doing the same things repeatedly. Most of us have seen or at least heard of the movie Groundhog Day, where Bill Murray experiences the same day repeatedly. There is some definite truth to the plot of that movie and the field of sales is certainly not immune to that. You wake up, go to work, sell the same things, deal with the same objections, and so on. So how do you break that pattern and avoid the ever-popular term "burn out." I believe the answer to that is fairly simple-have some fun!

Too many people still live with the idea that work is work and fun is fun, and the two shall not mix. However, if work can also be fun, do you think people would be more productive? The field of sales is competitive, as we all know but that same competitiveness can also make it fun. Let us say you are in the business of selling computers and you notice that your salespeople just seem a little drained and seem to be going through the motions. How about rather than giving another motivational speech that will probably only last an hour or two; you try something different this time.

Let's play a game! I am not talking about sales competition where the winner wins a trip but rather a game where the winner wins something as simple as a free lunch or the privilege to leave an hour early that day. For example, the salesperson that sells the most monitors in a given day gets free lunch for the rest of the week. Are you thinking to yourself this is childish and people should not need this type of motivation? It is not about motivation, it is about taking the everyday grind, and breaking it up and letting people have some fun. Trust me you will be pleasantly surprised at the results and the increase in sales. People, especially salespeople, are naturally competitive and little games as described above are a great tool in combating the day-to-day blahs that we all feel from time to time.

It's the little details that are vital. Little things make big things happen.

John Wooden

It's all About the Coffee!

We have talked numerous times over the years about customer services and the standards for which we should be striving. There is never a time when customer service standards should be compromised or sacrificed for something else. I am not going to spend time going over the standards of customer service but what I do want to do is emphasize the importance of those standards in today's world.

Take a minute and look around at what is happening. People are busier now than they have ever been before and people have more choices for their goods and services than ever. Every time I turn around, there is another company offering to refinance my mortgage or another company that can make my grass greener. In short, people have so many choices and your job is to make sure that you are the choice more often than not. Once again, this is certainly not a new concept and we have discussed it numerous times in the past but I had a reminder lately of how important those standards of customer service are.

Gas prices are high everywhere and I understand that local gas stations have little to no control over those prices but that does not mean their customer service should suffer. I recently purchased gas twice in two days. The first day, I went to a station where the price was a little higher than the place across the street but I was in a hurry and it was easier to get in and out of this particular station. The person working there was friendly and even told me that if I purchased at least twenty dollars of gas, then I would be eligible for a free coffee or bottle of pop. It may not sound like much but for a guy who forgot his coffee at home, it was a nice surprise.

The next day as I went to fill up my wife's car, I thought about going across the street because it was a little cheaper. Then I remembered the service that I had received from the other place the day before and I found myself turning in there almost without even thinking about it. I think that sometimes we forget that most people, while they want the best deal possible, want to be treated right and made to feel special. One free cup of coffee made me forget the high price of gas, if only for a moment.

"If passion drives you, let reason hold the reins."

\- *Benjamin Franklin*

PASSION

A few Saturdays ago, my wife and I were out and about running a bunch of different errands and trying to get some business taken care of. I am sure you know the feeling; you keep saying I can do that later and then it is much later, and you need to get a million things done in one day. Well it was one of those types of days, so we just decided to take a Saturday and get it all done in one swoop.

As we were running our errands and going in and out of different businesses, I began to notice some themes, especially when it came to the salespeople (occupational hazard, I guess). The one thing that I noticed that really interested me was between the salespeople who seem to be trying too hard and the ones that were just being themselves and "going with the flow." My wife and I were looking for a new stereo system for our car so we went and looked at a few different retailers. Now as you probably know, every electronic store offers pretty much the same thing. Often the salesperson makes the difference.

The first salesperson that we interacted with was nice enough and certainly knew his stuff including: features, inventory, prices and so on but there just seemed to be something missing that I could not put my finger on until we reached the next store. The salesperson at the second store offered the exact same information but did so in a way that got me excited to buy from them. After making the purchase from the second store, I started to think about what was different in the approaches of the two salespeople. Then it hit me, the first salesperson while competent and knowledgeable lacked energy, and a passion for the job. The salesperson was almost robotic in going through the presentation whereas, the second salesperson was genuinely excited to help us and his passion for what he was selling is the thing that sold us. Of course people have to be who they are and you should never fake enthusiasm but it is a lot more fun for the customer if the salesperson enjoys what they are doing. Some jobs work without passion; I do not believe sales are one of them.

Competition is not only the basis of protection to the customer; it is the incentive towards progress.

Herbert Hoover

MYSTERY SHOPPING – PART 0NE

We have talked time and again about the importance of taking advantage of every tool and every edge that you can find in the sales business. We discussed the importance of being prepared and preparing for everyday and we have talked about how effective it can be to use daily events to increase your customer base. The common thread through all of this is the importance of leaving no stone unturned and to be able to access and use every tool at your disposal.

There is one tool out there that is not used nearly enough, mystery shopping, and salespeople are missing out on this valuable asset. Mystery shopping is a technique, when mastered, can be the difference between the average salesperson and the salesperson that spends their vacations in exotic destinations. Mystery shopping, in its simplest form, is the practice of learning what your competitors are doing and how you compare to them. Think about it for a minute, football teams spend hours-watching film on their opponents. Why do they do this? The answer is very simple; they are looking for every edge they can find.

There are a few basics to mystery shopping and it should be noted that it is not difficult to do it just takes time. The purest form of mystery shopping is simply going into the stores of your competitors and shopping. Think about all of the things you can learn just by walking around the store of your competition: prices, level of customer service, product placement and the number of people in the store. Now all of this information by itself means very little but when you compare your findings to those same variables in your store, you begin to learn a great deal. Are your prices higher or lower? How does your level of customer service compare? If the outcomes are favorable, great you know you are on a good track. If the results are less favorable, then you can start to make the necessary adjustments.

Coaches in the NFL copy from each other all the time and it is not cheating, it is smart. If a team is winning with a certain type of offense, you can safely bet that other teams will begin to incorporate some of that offense into their offense. Next time, we will talk about what to do with the information that we obtain from mystery shopping.

To be prepared against surprise is to be trained.

To be prepared for surprise is to be educated.

James Carse

MYSTERY SHOPPING – PART TWO

Last time we started talking about mystery shopping and the benefits of doing it. We also discussed the type of information that you will probably obtain by taking advantage of this tool. Today I want to continue by examining what to do with all of that information. There is nothing more valuable than data and information if one knows what to do with it; and information can be useless if not used correctly.

Chances are, no matter how great your business is, that there is someone doing something better than you are and this is where we go back to the idea of not being afraid to learn from your competitors. Let us say for example, that you discover you prefer a competitor's product placement to yours and you decide to make a change. Now, here is the point where people often make a mistake. Your business is exactly that, yours and you never want to sacrifice your personal touch.

The secret lies in taking good ideas from others, competitors in this case, and working them into YOUR system of doing things. Remember last week when we talked about how football coaches often copy stuff that works, they don't copy the entire offense and make it their own, but they do take pieces of it that they like and work it into their system. They may run the same passing play that another team runs, but they may run it from the other side of the field, or at a different point on the field. The key is improving the offense without disrupting the system you have developed.

The same is true in the field of sales. We talked earlier about liking the product placement of your competitor better, but how should you implement that idea into your business? Chances are that your store's layout is different and copying your competitor's product placement to the letter is probably impossible. What you can do though, is take the principles that made you like the product placement and apply them to your set-up. You have developed your customer base for a number of reasons and the biggest reason is the unique personality of both you and your business. Next time we will discuss some more in-depth aspects of mystery shopping.

Where observation is concerned, chance favors only the prepared man.

Louie Pasteur

MYSTERY SHOPPING – PART THREE

We have spent the last few weeks talking about mystery shopping at its most basic point, simply the idea of going out and shopping your competitors on your own. However, there are some more advance principles in mystery shopping that I would like to touch on.

One of the most common practices that businesses use, particularly larger ones, is a professional mystery shopper. They are exactly what they sound like, shoppers hired by a competitor of yours to shop in your store and report their results. The professional mystery shoppers will most likely have a specific set of things that they are looking for and they know how to look for them. They will ask salespeople questions designed to gauge the level of customer service and the salesperson's product knowledge. They may come up with objections to see how the salesperson will react. In short, they are to the sales field as a scout is to a head football coach. They know exactly what they are looking for and how to obtain it.

One way that you can have your own mystery shoppers do a better job than a professional mystery shopping service is for you to develop your own complete checklist of things you want shopped. You know you know your industry and market better than anyone else does. Develop the checklist looking for specific things that you want answered. For example, did they turn over the sale, attempt to show a specific item, did they ask add-on questions and so on.

Another way to mystery shop is simply to keep an eye on advertising, both paper and electronic. Look at the Sunday paper, for example, to see what specials your competitors are running and to gauge their prices in comparison to yours. Are their sale prices higher than your everyday prices? Are they running specials on items that you sell like hotcakes? There is no reason that you should not at least keep track of your competitors in this way. It is simple, not time consuming, and the cost is nothing. Mystery shopping, in any form, is a vital tool for professional salespeople. DO NOT LEAVE IT IN THE TOOLBOX

*Believe in your dreams and they may come true,
believe in yourself and they will.*

Unknown

Motivation

Have you ever been asked what your primary motivation is, or what motivated you to complete a particular task? How do you answer that question? My guess is that you often think for a minute and either come up with an answer that people want to hear or you simply say "I do not know why I did that." Relax, you are not alone. Motivation is something that we all talk about but very few of us can really define what it means to each of us, let alone what it means to others.

Motivation is an integral part of sales. Motivated salespeople are the ones who are going to see the best results. I am a firm believer that real motivation comes from within and if someone is not internally motivated, then all the motivational speeches and techniques in the world are not going to help. Most, if not all, salespeople do possess that internal sense of motivation and the job of any sales manager is to find out what motivates each person, and then use it.

You may have some salespeople who are only motivated by the commission that they will receive from whatever they sell; you may have others who are motivated by the relationships that they establish with their customers. Finally, you may have some who are motivated by the Mexico trip that goes to the top salesperson at the end of the year. The conversations that you have with each of these salespeople are going to differ greatly based on what their motivation is. You may remind the person who is motivated by sales goals what the all-time record is and that they have a shot at it if they push themselves. A thank-you note from a satisfied customer will probably motivate the salesperson who enjoys the relationships with customers, and a simple postcard of Mexico will probably be enough motivation for the other salesperson.

You get the idea; there are no magical techniques to motivation. You simply have to know the people that you work with to truly understand what motivates them so they will be the best they can be. Some people need a pat on the back and others may not need anything. Selling is like everything else, the more motivated the salesperson is, the better the results.

If a window of opportunity appears, don't pull down the shade.

Thomas J. Peters

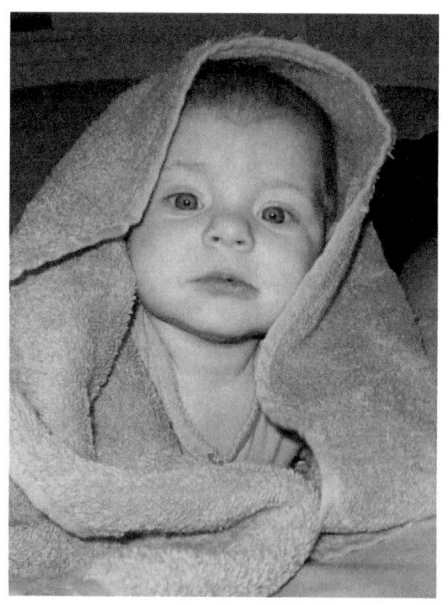

Maximize Every Opportunity!

In the next four to five weeks many of you will have more potential customers through your doors than at any other time during the year. For that matter you may have more potential customers through the doors in the next few weeks than you have even had come in so far this entire year. It is vitally important that each and every one of you maximize each selling opportunity.

During the holiday shopping season even the most seasoned "shoppers" become "buyers". Many people go from "Looky Lous" to "Hunters" on a mission to buy. This is especially true the nearer the holiday becomes. For that reason I thought I would devote this Sales Insight to questions that you can ask in order to help you maximize every selling opportunity. I have stated in the past, the primary way to maximize a sale is by adding-on. I assure you that you will be more successful if you start the adding-on process early in the presentation by asking these questions.

> Who is on your holiday gift giving list?
>
> What other special events do you have coming up?
>
> What does he/she have that they can wear with this?
>
> Tell me about his/her _____ wardrobe?
>
> What did you have in mind as a Valentine's Day gift?
>
> What else can I show you to help complete your Holiday Shopping?
>
> How about a perfectly matching _____ to complete his/her outfit?

These are just a few questions that you can use to start. There are just as many questions to ask, as there are selling situations. I would look at every situation and come up with your own list of add-on questions that work for you. The better the questions the more successful you will be. Remember, your job is to always think add-ons and to get your customer to think of buying more from you and your company. Remember adding-on *is* great customer service.

246

Space is to place as eternity is to time.

Joseph Joubert

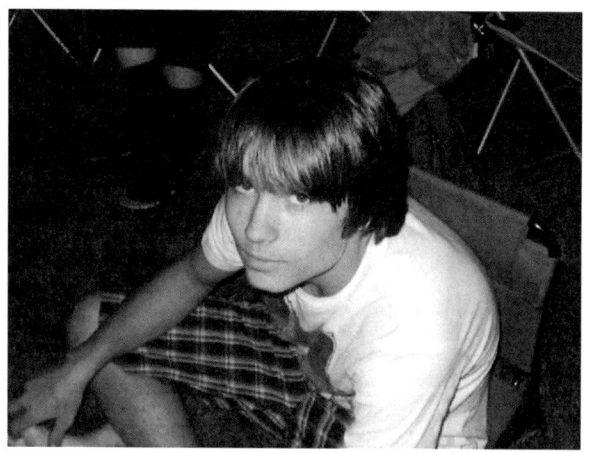

Personal Space

We talk a lot about how to meet our customer's needs and about being attentive. While it is always true that we need to be aware of our customer's wants and needs, it is just as important to respect the wishes of the customer. Have I completely confused you yet? What I am talking about today is the issue of personal space and having respect for the personal space of your customers.

The issue came up when I was doing a little shopping at an electronics store the other day. I was interested in a new computer for a family member and was just beginning to do some comparison shopping. If something really hit me or caught my eye, I was prepared to make the purchase that day but was in no hurry to do so. As I begin to talk with the salesperson, he starts with the usual small talk followed by his presentation about the specific computers that I am looking at. Everything is fine but I am not seeing what I want, so I politely tell the salesperson thank-you but I think I will keep looking. He hands me his business card and moves on, as do I, and then it happened. The salesperson proceeded to follow me over to the digital camera area and then to the DVD section. In each area, he would ask me if there was anything that he could show me. At this point, the salesperson is very annoying and I just simply left the store. We had a business conversation and it ended on a positive note but the salesperson failed to respect my personal space. In his pursuit to make a sale he not only lost a customer for the day, he also lost any chance of me coming back to buy that computer.

The message here is a simple one. Do your job and make your best presentation, but don't ever violate the personal space of your customers, and respect their decisions. We all feel uncomfortable to some degree when we feel our personal space is being compromised. So just remember to respect both your customer's personal space and the choices they make.

You must live in the present, launch yourself on every wave, and find your eternity in each moment.

Henry David Thoreau

Moments!

I would like to take a moment and talk about moments, those moments that make up what we call life. As I continue to grow older, no jokes here, I believe more and more that life is made up of all kinds of different moments or occasions. Our family has had a couple of weddings in the last month and another one in a couple of weeks. As I was sitting there, it dawned on me that this is what life should be about. My entire family was there having a good time and all of our day-to-day troubles were millions of miles away.

I am sure you are asking yourself at this point, what any of this has to do with the field of sales. The answer to that question potentially has many answers but for me, there are two specific ones that come to mind. The first is directly related to sales, especially for those who are selling high priced items or are in the business of selling emotional goods or goods that people are passionate about. For example, when a young man decides to buy an engagement ring for his girlfriend, moments do not get any bigger than this. If the salesperson is aware of this, then they have the potential to make not only one sale but also develop a customer for life. A lot of being a part of this moment has nothing to do with anything you show them or any kind of price break, but rather the way you interact with the customer. They are obviously excited about this purchase and all you have to do is share their excitement, share the moment with them.

The second thing I just want to touch on is simply the fact that the moments you have in your own life will make you a better salesperson. I know that after I went to those weddings and spent time with family celebrating I was refreshed and ready to go back to work on Monday. I am not here to give life lessons but I do believe that the moments and occasions that we live for make us better salespeople. As Lennon said in one of his songs – "Life is what happens while we plan the future."

Therefore, whether it is your moment or a customer's moment, embrace it, and let it help you become the best salesperson possible. Life is not about the next car payment due; it is about the next relative that does something worth celebrating.

*If I pick up the phone, I accept responsibility to
ensure the caller is satisfied, No matter what the
issue is.*

Michael Ramundo

PHONE CUSTOMER SERVICE

Recently I wrote about a nephew who has been working with people with disabilities for over fourteen years. I told you that part of his job involves scheduling rides for individuals with disabilities to get to and from their places of employment. In addition, where he lives there is only one company that provides this service and they have zero competition.

This leads me to the main point of the day and that is customer service via the telephone is just as important as any other form of customer service. My nephew has shared with me some stories that make me cringe, and he believes it is because they know that their customers have no other choice.

There are some key things to remember when speaking with a customer by phone.

- There is a potential customer/buyer on the other end of the line; they deserve the same respect and attention that you would give to a customer standing in front of you.
- Understand they are calling you to obtain specific information. They do not much care how busy you are. Always make sure that you are using a professional tone of voice and are not taking out a bad day on the caller. (It is easier to do when they are not standing right in front of you.)
- Have some idea of a presentation that will work over the phone. The goal when speaking with someone over the phone should be to do whatever it takes to get him or her in front of you and not one who could hang up on you at any point.
- Finally, have respect for people who call by not leaving him or her on hold any longer than necessary and give them the same attention you would give to every customer.
-

We live in a world where everyone is on the go and has a cell phone. Do not get left behind because your phone customer service is not up to par.

Spend a lot of time talking to customers face to face. You'd be amazed how many companies don't listen to their customers.

Ross Perot

Phone Phrustrations!

First impressions are without a doubt the most important impression that your customer has of you, that will cause them to choose to deal with you and hopefully make a purchase. Last impressions are just as important and those that will cause a customer or potential customer to come back and deal with you and/or your company again and again. In many instances the very first impression and/or the last impression that a potential customer has of you and your company could be the telephone.

Knowing this to be true, it amazes me how little attention is put on telephone manners, techniques and disciplines. I am forever calling companies where I have the privilege of listening to the long version of In-A-Gadda-Da-Vida whether I want to or not. Sarcasm aside, the length of time someone is left on hold shouldn't be any more than a minute or two. Certainly not the 5, 10, or even the 12 minutes that I have experienced lately. Being offered a connection to someone's voice mail and having the phone disconnect not once but two or three times is inexcusable. Having the person on the other end of the phone search for what seems like hours for a pen and paper to take a message is unacceptable. Having the telephone ring and ring and ring for ten to fifteen rings is aggravating at best. Having a rude, abrasive person answering the telephone with just the company name is offending. What happened to answering the phone with a nice salutation and offering the company name and the name of the person who answered the telephone? In other words, have some kind of personal interaction with the person on the other end of the line.

Maybe I am turning into my parents, but I still believe that people want to deal with a real, live, human being on the other end of a telephone. If I didn't want to talk to someone I would send a text or an e-mail. Call your store or company sometime and experience what your customers are experiencing. It might frighten some of you. The telephone can be a great tool or a terrible determent to your business.

254

*I worked hard at memorizing facts and figures,
and carried with me a book of facts.*

Charles Van Doren

Memorize Your Prices

We talk all the time about the differences between an average salesperson and a great salesperson. We have discussed that the small things are what separates the average salesperson from the great ones. One of those things we covered in our last Sales Insight, the importance of not only knowing your inventory but also having a working knowledge of it on a daily basis. Along those same lines, it is also vital that you memorize the prices of the items that you are selling.

That may sound easier than it is because, as your inventory can change on a daily basis, so can the prices of what you are selling. Especially as we enter the holiday season, which is, the busiest time of the year in terms of shopping. It is important that you take the time to memorize your prices and are able to draw upon that memory in a moment's notice. You may ask why it is such a big deal; I mean it only takes a minute or two to look it up. When your store or business is busy, as you hope it will be, then minutes here and there are huge.

People who are holiday shopping are many times rushed for time and have many other things that have to be done. When a salesperson says, "Wait here one minute and I will go look up that price," the customer is likely to become frustrated and begin looking at their watch. By the time the salesperson returns with the price, chances are good that the customer has either lost interest of left all together. On the other hand, if a salesperson is able to rattle off the prices of whatever it is that they are interested in, then you are more likely to keep their attention and complete the sale.

We live in a fast-paced society and if a salesperson is able to keep the conversation with their customer's upbeat and moving, then it makes for a more positive selling environment. A lot of selling, as we all know, is based on the relationships and trust that you are able to build with your customers. If you are knowledgeable of your prices and all that goes with that including sales and discounts, then you have started the process of building relationships that lead to repeat customers and setting yourself apart from the average salesperson.

The purpose of a business is to create a mutually beneficial relationship between itself and those that it serves. When it does that well, it will be around tomorrow to do more of the same.

John Woods

RELATIONSHIPS SELL

I recently went to a baseball game with a couple of friends; one of those friends is a salesperson who specializes in setting up computer networks for small companies. As we watched the game, we began talking with the people around us, and what happened next just goes to show you that relationships and networking are often more important than the product you are selling.

My friend, the salesperson, started a conversation with the person next to him about the game and baseball in general and whatever else happened to come up. As they continued talking, their conversation turned to business. As it turns out, the person with whom he was talking had just started a small company and had begun looking for a computer/networking system.

My friend started telling him about all the different options that he could offer and how they could tailor a system that would fit his business and fit his start up budget. At first, the customer was interested but just not sure it was a good idea to be making this large of decision at a Friday night baseball game. He asked my friend for his card and said he would think about it and maybe give him a call.

Their conversation turned back to the pitching in the game and they discussed the possibility that a change in order on the mound. As the night progressed, you could just sense they were fast becoming friends. By the eighth inning, their conversation made its way back to business and this time the new business owner was ready to talk specifics and possibly make a purchase from his new friend. Two weeks later, I asked if he had made a sale to the person at the baseball game. He told me that it was the biggest sale he had ever made.

The point of this is not to prove that my friend is a great salesperson or that a baseball game is the ultimate spot for a salesperson to make a living. The point of this story is just to remind you that establishing relationships is very often more important than the product you are selling. Sure, there has to be a need for what you are selling, but the relationship between the salesperson and the customer is what sells the product. My guess is that my friend and his new customer will be doing business together for a long time, and it is all because of a relationship they established at a baseball game.

Nobody can stop you from choosing to be exceptional.

Mark Sanborn

Make the Follow-Up Personal

We have always talked about the importance of follow up calls and thank you notes. I shared with you a couple of examples of follow up gone wrong. I would like to share with you some examples of following up with customers that were executed in a very professional and timely manner.

After my son purchased a car and had it for a while, he continued to be extremely happy the purchase and even told some friends about the incredible service that he had received. A couple of weeks went by and he received a phone call from the primary salesperson. In a number of ways it was a standard follow up call, how do you like your new car, and do you have any questions and so on. What separated this call and what made it stand out were many little things.

The first was that he remembered a number of facts about his wife, but also our relatives. After he had discussed the specifics to the car, the salesperson asked about his work. It was obvious and impressive that he remembered what my son did for a living. Maybe impressive is the wrong word, but that question certainly made him feel less like a person who gave him a commission and more like a friend that he would like to do business with again in the future.

He also asked about how a school play that my daughter-in-law was supervising as a teacher. In the course of our conversation, we had mentioned to him that we were excited the play that same night. The fact that he remembered that in the course of selling us a car really said something to me. Yes, he wants to sell a car but he is also genuinely interested in what they had told him.

In addition, they also received similar follow up calls from the service manager, who took the time to outline a maintenance schedule and even offered the first oil change free. Following up on a completed sale is one of the best ways to develop relationships with customers that will last longer than one sale. I know when they are in need of another car, this salesperson will be the first one that they viit.

If you're not using your smile, you're like a man with a million dollars in the bank and no checkbook.

Les Giblin

It Only Takes A Second!

It doesn't take but a second to separate yourself from what seems like, the majority of people in the sales and service industries. As a matter of fact it probably doesn't take any more time to just be nice than it does to be average. I assure you the time it takes to be nice will make all the difference in the world in the feelings that people leave with.

I was recently on a long flight where the flight attendants didn't seem to be any happier about being there than I was. The attendants weren't necessarily rude, they were just there. They served the drinks, served the meal, not many smiles, and absolutely no personal interaction. In reality they were just fixtures of the airplane. Yet, on another short flight I had recently, I met a very warm and personable flight attendant. When I got on the plane she said, "Hello, how are you today?" She went on to introduce herself by saying, "My name is Shannon what's yours?" I introduced myself at that point and took my seat. She then stated that she would be happy to get me something to drink as soon as we take off and if there is anything she can do to let her know. Basically, she was just being a warm friendly person who appeared to enjoy her job and at the very least makes the flight more pleasant for everyone involved. Prior to take-off I dozed off and never got the drink, I would guess that she didn't want to disturb me. After a short time I woke up and noticed she had put a pillow in my lap. Great extra effort that took no more time than it would have to ignore me.

It doesn't take any more time to be pleasant, warm, friendly and caring than it does to be melancholy. However, the difference it will make in the customer's mind is dramatic. Make dealing with you a pleasant experience and customers will proactively come back to you. Be just average and you really don't know if they will come back or not. Being nice just might make more sales for you and cause your company to be a more pleasant place to work and buy.

When ye are prepared for a thing, the opportunity
to use it presents itself.

Edgar Cavce

Homework!

For all of those who have school age kids, you already know that school has resumed and the routine of homework, practices, and group activities has begun its cycle once again. What I want to focus on today is the homework, and I am not talking about your daughter's math.

Selling is more than just showing up on the days you work and just start selling. If it were that simple, everyone would be doing it for a living. Granted professional salespeople are very talented and the best at what they do but the very best are the ones that do their homework. What kind of homework am I referring to?

The most important homework a salesperson can perform is knowing the product they are selling inside and out. Of course, we all take the time to learn our product when we first begin or when a new product comes out, but it is those who do their continual homework that are the most successful. Every salesperson should begin each and every day by reviewing the products they sell and what, if any, changes have been made to the product. Most of the time there probably will not be any changes, but by doing your daily homework, you will assure yourself that you will not miss changes when they occur.

Another part of a salesperson's homework is being aware of any specials or sales that your store has going on currently. These are probably going to change fairly often, so it is vital that you take time each day to remind yourself of what products are discounted and what products are currently offering a free extended warranty. Offers like these are there to help you satisfy the customer and his/her needs, so they are counting on you to be able to tell them what the deals are and how they best fit the customer's needs.

The word homework often conjures up bad memories in a lot of us, but for those of us in the field of sales, it is necessary if we want to reach the top of our profession. A football team cannot show up on opening day and play, a student cannot show up on the day of the ACT test and pass. A salesperson cannot show up and start selling to their maximum potential. They all require one thing--HOMEWORK!

It's not the employer who pays the wages.
Employers only handle the money. It's the
customer who pays the wages.

Henry Ford

More Doom & Gloom – How Lucky are We?

Watching CNN this morning, I heard the latest report on retail sales for the month. Sales were off significantly. The Gap reported a loss of 18%, Target was off 9%, and Linens and Things are on the brink of bankruptcy. CNN stated that Linens & Things would probably be closing stores and eliminating up to 17,000 jobs. Overall, it sounds like the end is near.

Upon hearing this news, I just thought how lucky are we, that as independent, professional retail sales organizations, we do not have to depend on retail **clerks** to make or break our companies. All of my clients and most that receive this newsletter are sales driven organizations with sales people that are hired to turn shoppers into buyers. We do not have to depend on clerks for sales; we have professionals. I remember asking a storeowner how many salespeople he had – jokingly (I think) he said, "None, but I have twelve employees." That is scary!

I was with a store last week that is running up 18% for the year – another store is having the best year ever, some are breaking even, and others are facing very serious sales losses. What is the difference? In many cases it boils down to the sales staff. Are they trained to be finely tuned sales professionals? Let me give you some warning signs that your sales staff needs help. Are they still saying can I help you – Will that be all – Here's my card - taking in a repair and not showing merchandise – not capturing name, address, phone number and permission for follow-up – not following up with a phone call or an email, - accepting "I'll be back" – not having a strong Turnover Program – don't sell based on the reasons a customer wants to buy as opposed to the reason they want to sell – doesn't increase trust through selling the store – doesn't understand that value is a perception and how to increase a customer's perception – doesn't make it a quest to develop personal trade with every customer – isn't asking for referrals – mentioning price before value has been established – isn't asking add-on questions – doesn't focus on the emotional side of the purchase – and so on…

A salesperson's job is to:

Cause: The exchange of ownership of a product or service, based on the customer's **wants** and **needs** with **integrity!**

Whose job is it to make sure the sales staff is fully trained in order to guarantee the company's success in the area of sales and profits? Frankly, it is responsibility of the owner and/or the sales manager. As long as you have competition in your area, you have an opportunity for a sales increase bottom line. I hope in five years you are not thought of the same way as Woolworth's and the many others who have followed.

266

*With ordinary talent and extraordinary
perseverance, all things are attainable.*

Thomas Foxwell Buxton

PERSEVERANCE

Today I do not want to talk about sales techniques, closing strategies, non-business conversations, or customer service standards. No, today I want to talk about something that everyone can do no matter what his or her experience or his or her skill level. It all boils down to one idea and, more importantly, one word. That word is perseverance. Simply stated, those who persevere will usually find success.

I just finished watching Dale Earnhardt, Jr. win a NASCAR race and it inspired me to sit down and write an article on the importance of never quitting. I do not pretend to know a lot about car racing but I do know that Earnhardt is a big name and that he has been struggling for the first time in his career. I remember watching an interview with him a couple of weeks ago, he impressed me with his determination and "whatever it takes" attitude to get his season turned around. In short, he persevered and finished third the week after the interview that I mentioned earlier and won the following week. Now his season appears to be back on track and the sheer joy he exhibited following the race was inspiring.

What does a NASCAR race have to do with the field of sales and the people who work in that field? The answer is not much except for the perseverance and determination that was on display. Like Earnhardt, we have all had those days when everyone says no and every lead is colder than winter in the North Pole, but the professional salesperson fights through those episodes. They keep selling and trying to turn those cold leads into "I'll take it!" If every customer said yes and you reached your quota every day, then everybody would be in the field of sales. The truth is, and you all already know this, that sales is about putting a lot of poles into the water and hoping a few of them hit.

I will think about it and *maybes* are responses that we all hear, probably more than we would like to admit. As Dale Earnhardt, Jr. has proven, if you hang in there and you persevere, anything is possible. He went from a lost season to a season of hope and it was, in large part, because he refused to give it less than his best effort. When you are having a rough day or a rough stretch, just remember to persevere.

Quality is remembered long after price is forgotten.

Gucci Family Slogan

Low Prices Do Not Replace Customer Service!

We have been spending a lot of time lately talking about customer service in a variety of different aspects. This week is no different, as I have another point regarding customer service that I find myself compelled to make.

We all understand the society we live in today, gas prices going up, food prices rising and the trickledown effect that those two things cause. Therefore, we are always looking for deals, any way to get what we need and find a way to save money at the same time. Businesses, some of them anyway, are trying to take advantage of this dynamic by running sales and specials designed to offer the customer a "helping hand." There is nothing wrong with that thinking. In fact, it is a good business practice to take what is going on in the world, and find a way to increase your sales and customer base.

Having said that, nothing, not even low prices, takes the place of providing quality customer service. Low prices and specials may bring customers in once, but lousy customer service will drive them away forever. I was recently in a store shopping and they were having an incredible sale on almost everything. The deals were great and I'll admit that we took full advantage of the opportunity. The problem was the customer service we received was some of the worst I have ever witnessed and I would not go back, even if those deals were still going.

There is the rub! The deals and the great buys eventually go away and eventually the customer forgets about the 5 bucks they saved on that lamp that broke two years ago. They do, however, remember the time they asked a salesperson to assist them with a large item and the salesperson said, "Do you think I have time to help you?" I am not joking, that actually happened. Another instance occurred when I inquired about where the hardware section was and the salesperson sighed and said, "You know we have signs?"

Sure, the money we saved was great but on the drive home, that is not what we discussed. We focused on the attitude and obvious lack of caring for the customers from the salespeople. I am sure they did a great business on that day but I often wonder how they did in the following days. Do not forget-nothing, NOTHING, replaces high-quality customer service!

You don't close a sale; you open a relationship if you want to build a long-term, successful enterprise.

Patricia Fripp

See The Sale All The Way To The End!

Last week we briefly discussed the importance of developing friendships after the sale. Today, I would like to talk about simply taking care of your end of the deal all the way to the end of the transaction. Keep in mind that I realize in many cases the salesperson is not at fault for mistakes made. However, I believe that the customer does hold the salesperson responsible. Let me provide an example to better illustrate my point. I recently shared with you the story of my friends that purchased a new mini van and some of the pitfalls that they encountered. Today, I would like to return to that example and talk about some of the things that did not happen after the sale that should have.

The first thing that happened was the fact that my friends received calls on three different occasions because the dealership could not get the financing papers right. I understand that mistakes happen, but it is inexcusable for a customer who has already made a purchase to be constantly bothered with callbacks because someone in finance, or maybe the salesperson, makes mistakes. Secondly, once they got the financing right they didn't bother to tell my friends and by the time they knew about it, their first payment was already two days late. Not that this is the end of the world but a late payment is not the start you want with a new creditor either. The final thing was that because of all the delays with the paperwork, no one from the dealership bothered to pay off the trade-in. Then my friends start getting letters and calls about why they are two months behind on their car payment. They did not make the payments because, obviously, they had traded that car in. They had to call the dealership to get them to send the pay off which is not their responsibility.

The bottom line is this if you care enough to sell something to someone then you should care enough to follow the sale all the way through the end of the transaction. Mistakes happen, but in many cases if the salesperson takes a little responsibility, the mistakes can be resolved before they become mistakes.

This may seem simple, but you need to give customers what they want, not what you think they want. If you do this, people will keep coming back.

John Ilhan

LIFE LONG CUSTOMER SERVICE

When we discuss the field of sales, no matter what we are talking about, somehow it always comes back to customer service. It does not matter what you are selling or how much your product costs. Customer service, it seems, is always a main factor that determines where a customer finally buys from, and returns to shop. It occurred to me the other day though, that maybe we think of customer service too much in the present and not enough in future terms. I would like to share a story with you about a friend and his dog to help me illustrate my point.

My buddy has had his dog for as long as I have known him, and has used the same vet for the same period of time. Over the years he raved about his vet and how well they treated his dog, and how the service he received was second to none. He talked about the time that his dog was very sick. He could not afford the medical treatment but the vet agreed to a monthly payment plan, even though there was no guarantee that the dog would get better. Thankfully, everything worked out and after a couple of years, the dog was healthy and happy and the bill was gone. This is only one of many examples of how the vet worked with my friend and provided the customer service that was second to none.

In the last couple of years though, I'm sorry to say, that level of service has declined and sometimes rapidly. There was a time right around the holidays last year when my friend's dog was in need of medication. However, my friend just had bigger needs of his own at the time. Even though he had ALWAYS paid the vet in a timely manner and owed them no money at the time, they refused to let him make payments. In the end, my friend found a way to buy the medication and to this day, he and his dog are as close as ever, with a new vet.

The lesson here is simple: customer service does not end after a customer has been a customer for a set period of time. Customer service never ends; and a professional salesperson never takes any customer, new or repeat, for granted.

FINAO

Failure Is Not An Option!